Sze Sze, My Daughter

by
Bill Van Dam

Copyright © 2012 by Bill Van Dam

Sze Sze, My Daughter
by Bill Van Dam

Printed in the United States of America

ISBN 9781622307883

All rights reserved solely by the author. The author guarantees all contents are original and do not infringe upon the legal rights of any other person or work. No part of this book may be reproduced in any form without the permission of the author. The views expressed in this book are not necessarily those of the publisher.

Unless otherwise indicated, Bible quotations are taken from the New International Version of the Bible. Copyright © 1985 by the Zondervan Corporation.

www.xulonpress.com

This book is dedicated to
Valerie Conibear
and
Wendy Blackmur
who have made me see and treasure
the Lord's "riches stored in secret places."
Isaiah 43:3

Table of Contents

Chapter 1 11
In which we are introduced to Sze Sze, Auntie Ena and Uncle Bill. After a three-month swing through China, a retired couple from Canada reluctantly visits the Home of Loving Faithfulness in Hong Kong. It proves to be a life changing visit for them and Sze Sze.

Chapter 2 16
On their second visit to the home, Uncle Bill and Auntie Ena get to know the family better. Uncle Bill learns to communicate with Sze Sze and begins to explore better ways for her to express herself.

Chapter 3 25
The SARS outbreak causes uncertainty about returning to Hong Kong. Relying on modern technology, many years of teaching experience and Sze Sze's enthusiasm, Uncle Bill begins teaching her, but he soon realizes that the task he has undertaken is more difficult than he anticipated.

Chapter 4 34
Uncle Bill and Auntie Ena discover a weakness in the spiritual nurture of the family and begin a ministry of evening devotions with the family. Sze Sze expresses the desire to receive baptism, and preparations for her baptism prove to be emotional . . . and revealing. Sze Sze is discouraged because after three months of instruction she is still unable to read or write.

Chapter 5 45
Uncle Bill and Auntie Ena receive an unfriendly welcome when they return from Hong Kong. Uncle Bill suffers a heart attack and makes a difficult recovery.

Chapter 6 51
Upon their return to Hong Kong, Uncle Bill and Auntie Ena discover they have the whole lower deck of the Ark as their living quarters. Protecting the dignity of family members: carried out consistently or selectively? Computer problems cause teaching to get off on a rough start. Uncle Bill proposes a different approach to reading, Sze Sze is skeptical, but we make a significant breakthrough.

Chapter 7 62
Despite her multiple handicaps, Sze Sze has the same interests, concerns, fears and spiritual ups and downs as 'normal' people. She adds to her collection of time pieces. Sze Sze continues to struggle in spelling; Uncle Bill wonders if he's up against a roadblock or a mental block. Sze Sze blames fear of failure; Uncle Bill thinks it is fear of the unknown. Sze Sze finds out it is sometimes alright to be angry with God.

Chapter 8 74
Auntie Ena and Uncle Bill feel redundant when they are home in Canada, and time at home becomes maintenance time for Uncle Bill. Sze Sze exhibits some unacceptable behavior and needs to be confronted. Uncle Bill struggles with questions regarding Sze Sze's intelligence and intellectual development. A new approach to spelling proves to be less than an overwhelming success. Uncle Bill searches for a better way for Sze Sze to access her computer.

Chapter 9 90
Kim suffers a stroke, and Sze Sze is hospitalized because of a recurrence of an old problem. She undergoes two serious operations and hovers on the brink of death. Ten thousand kilometers away, Uncle Bill experiences his Peniel. He also reflects on the 2004 Boxing Day earthquake of the coast off Sumatra and resulting *tsunami*.

Chapter 10 96
Auntie Ena and Uncle Bill return to Hong Kong to be with Sze Sze. For two and a half weeks they visit her every day. Sze Sze's recovery is slow and uneven. After almost three months she returns home.

Chapter 11 110
Sze Sze battles flu bugs and private demons. We deal with rivalry between Dib Dib and Sze Sze. Sze Sze regains strength but is

Sze Sze, My Daughter

reluctant to resume studies. Sze Sze's laptop has disappeared and is replaced. Uncle Bill renews efforts to find a way for Sze Sze to access her computer. Co Co proves to be an answer to prayer. Uncle Bill asks Sze Sze some sensitive questions. Sandy is arrested.

Chapter 12 132
Sze Sze has made good physical recovery but needs emotional and spiritual healing. She reveals a vision of heaven she received when in hospital. Uncle Bill and Sze Sze become discouraged and Sze Sze throws in the towel—for a while. We celebrate Sze Sze's twenty-first birthday. Mother, I love you, but . . . . Sze Sze in love—not again! During a visit to Hong Kong Disneyland, Sze Sze receives injury. Sze Sze and her father, Uncle Bill touches upon a difficult subject. Happy New Year, daughter.

Epilogue 149
Sze Sze, Shaan, Dibs and Fung Tai become part of a new family unit in the Lower Ark. The new house mother and Sze Sze go through a time of adjustment. Because of fear of aspirated pneumonia, Sze Sze is put on tube feeding. Life begins to lose color for Sze Sze. She loses interest in reading but wants to be read to. Sze Sze tries to starve herself. She goes through another lengthy and painful hospitalization. Uncle Bill makes suggestions for new leader of the home to meet unmet needs. He takes time to reflect and give thanks.

Chapter 1

Sze Sze[1] must have been a beautiful, perfectly formed baby and the pride of her parents. A picture, taken long before she came to live in the home, shows her seated in a stroller: bright-eyed, confidently looking into the world, a place filled with challenges and frustrations, not yet realizing what life had in store for her. I first met her as a teenager, a proud one it seemed, checking me out from a distance. She intrigued me. After we had become close friends, I once asked her what her first impression of me had been. I shouldn't have. She merely laughed, softly, throwing back her head, teasing without telling.

At 17, when we first met, Sze Sze's beauty wasn't stunning, making men's heads turn when they passed her. Women in wheelchairs don't get a second look, just a quick glance. Although her face is attractive and her smile winning, it is her eyes that define her, reveal her true self and set her apart. They lack even a hint of the inferiority and insecurity that mark many of those who are physically disabled. They reveal a keen and observant mind, watching people with curiosity, frankness and even, at times, defiance. They reflect deep-seated emotions, smoldering when angry, mocking when disdainful, questioning when puzzled, heartwarming when joyful and overwhelming when gazing at the object of her love.

Her slight, flat-chested body lacks muscle tone and is scarred and scored by surgeons' scalpels. It will never grace swim wear editions of fashion magazines. Her slender neck, hidden by a brace covering her chest, shoulders and sides of her face, is unable to support the weight of her head.

Sze Sze's is an inner beauty. It radiates strength of character forged in the furnace of adversity, illness, pain and discomfort. Adversity struck when she was but a baby, stopping her heart, starving her of oxygen in the part of her brain that controls her muscles, rendering them useless, leaving her spastic and unable to speak. Illness brought her near enough to death to see heaven's gate swing open only to see it slammed shut again. Pain is a close companion, discomfort no stranger. Affliction, like an artisan's hammer, has molded her character to be strong and resilient. Suffering, rather than squelching her spirit, has burnished its beauty.

Those who take time to know Sze Sze discover an intelligence impatient to burst forth from the prison of her unresponsive body; even those who spend little time with her find a young woman who follows discussions with interest and understanding. Her keen intuition picks up on incongruities creating humorous situations, and her perceptive mind catches subtle word plays, both in her native Cantonese and English.

Sze Sze and I first met in the home in Kwu Tung, in December 2001. Kwu Tung is a village just outside Sheung Shui, one of Hong Kong's satellite cities, the second last stop before coming to the Mainland China border, on what used to be called the KCR Line, and the last stop on our three-month trek through China.

Perhaps I should backtrack and tell how it all happened. In 1996, my wife Ena and I retired from six years of teaching English in China, a country that holds for us many precious memories. We were unable to forget our numerous Chinese friends, and we often looked for an excuse to return to the Middle Kingdom[2]. An opportunity presented itself in the spring of 2001 in the form of a wedding invitation. Liu Jianxing and Sun Yufang, two students I had taught at Laiyang Agricultural College in the Shandong Province, wrote that they would be greatly honored if Bill *Loa shi*,[3] their teacher and matchmaker, and Ena, his *tai tai*,[4] would attend their wedding celebrations planned for China's Golden Week.[5] We gladly accepted. We set September 11 as our day of departure from Canada, but the violent events of that day, seared forever in the memory of the Western world, prevented our leaving on that day.

In Tokyo, the first stop on our way to China, we visited our youngest son, his wife and their son Willem, my namesake. Terence had followed in his parents' footsteps and was teaching English abroad. In Japan he had met Christy who, like St. Francis Xavier, was heeding the call to spread the gospel in the Land of the Rising Sun.

While she was a student at Anderson University, Christy had volunteered a number of months in the Home of Loving Faithfulness, a most wonderful place, she assured us. She encouraged us to visit it when we would be in Hong Kong. When I asked, "Tell me, Christy, what is so attractive about that place?" she gushed, "Oh, it's . . . it's simply wonderful! You can give the kids rides in their wheelchairs in the garden, and you can help feed them, and there are lots of other things you can do there," without elaborating on what those other things were. Neither pushing wheelchairs nor feeding disabled people was part of our previous experience, nor did those activities hold any attraction for us. However, we wanted to please our daughter-in-law, so we asked her to find out if a visit to the home would be welcomed. We secretly hoped she would forget and quietly wished the home would be too busy to entertain reluctant visitors. We had no such luck. Three weeks later in China, checking my e-mail, I found in my Inbox an invitation from the home. It was complete with instructions on how to get there and informed us that a room had been reserved for us. It barred all hope of evasion.

We received a warm welcome from the Aunties. In 1965, Wendy Blackmur and Valerie Conibear, moved by the plight of severely disabled children existing in backrooms of Hong Kong orphanages, had opened their hearts and the doors of a small bungalow in Fanling to create a home for those 'rejects' of society. We were pleasantly surprised by the atmosphere in the Home of Loving Faithfulness, a place almost too good to be true. There we found harmonious relationships, met happy care givers, discovered a home rather than an institution and were surrounded by family members instead of residents. We had discovered a place living up to its name. Its ambiance kept us from becoming overwhelmed by finding so many severely disabled people in one place.

We spent five days at the home, days that went by in a blur. We were awed by the positive impressions created by the friendliness of its staff, moved by the loving care given to the family and, yes, enamored by the enjoyment of interacting with the family. We left the home feeling we were family. We promised to return soon.

Our visit to the home was the beginning of a new and lasting relationship, a special bond between Sze Sze and me. Ours was not a first-sight kind of love. It was a devotion, opening like a rosebud, displaying new layers of loveliness at each stage, slowly coming to full bloom. Nor was it a passing infatuation. It was an evolving emotion, maturing to a rare affection, built on complete trust and mutual respect—a deep friendship between a girl about to become a woman and a retired teacher.

Sze Sze, My Daughter

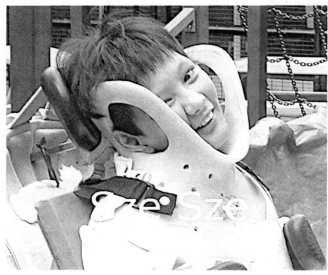

Sze Sze

Looking back over the past ten years, I ask myself how it all came about, this involvement in the life of a young woman, severely disabled and living half a world away. I wondered why I thought it worthwhile to spend so much time, my golden years, and money, carefully saved and wisely invested, and tireless effort and emotional energy to work with her.

The how-part is the most easily answered: An all-wise God took a retired special needs teacher, retreaded him, led him to a wonderful place and brought him face to face with one of his special creations to enrich her life—and his.

The why-part is more difficult to answer. My work with Sze Sze was motivated by a mix of professional and personal—or was it emotional?—interests. This young woman confronted me with problems I never before encountered and possibilities I never before tried. This new relationship necessitated new and better ways of communication. This new interaction revealed how normal—how much like all of us—she really is. It challenged the teacher in me.

Our friendship also awakened in me a new awareness. Many, seeing Sze Sze physically disabled and assuming her intellectually challenged as well, often treat her and others like her, in demeaning or patronizing ways that deeply troubled me. It made me want people to look at Sze Sze and others like her as I see her: with new eyes—or, perhaps, the same eyes they use to look at so-called normal people. I want them to see image bearers bruised by the fall but deserving of dignity and respect.

Chapter 2

As we had promised, we returned to the home in the spring of the following year. Ena got to know the kids, as we lovingly called them, better by helping them with their meals, taking them to the spacious, well-maintained garden surrounding the home or just having good times with them. I spent six weeks fixing kitchen cabinets, mending dresser drawers, putting up shelves and working on whatever needed improvement. I also discovered Emmanuel's delightful giggles, Fu Fu's infectious laughter and Fa Fa's radiant smiles. I learned about Wat Siu Ping's enjoyment of music and Shaan Shaan's love of people and the outdoors, no matter what the weather or time of day. I found out about Dib's exuberant exterior, hiding a sensitive soul, a spirit easily hurt and sometimes given to jealousy. I delighted in Ngan Ying's knowing smiles, reminding me to take "time to wait till her mouth can/Enrich that smile her eyes began."[6]

In Sze Sze and Yin Fan, I found bright minds trapped in unresponsive bodies, prisoners of dysfunctional muscles, nerves and sinews, Sze Sze more so than Yin Fan. The latter was an able speller and used a communication board ever so slowly but effectively; the former possessed neither the motor skills nor, I discovered later, the language proficiency needed to use such a device.

Time abroad always seems to pass faster than back home, and soon we found ourselves back in Canada. I explored ways to enrich the lives of those two young women, to widen their horizons, to add to their experiences, real or vicarious. I looked into means by which Yin Fan could access an e-book reader, but before our return to the home the following autumn, Someone Else had improved the quality of Yin Fan's life, enriching it more abundantly than I could have ever dreamt or imagined. She was 23 when the Lord set her free and took her home.

After Yin Fan's release from the bondage of her body, I began to spend more time with Sze Sze. I discovered I had been wrong in my initial assessment of her, mistaking caution for pride. Eventually

Sze Sze, My Daughter

I learned the reason for her wariness. I was often asked to feed Sze Sze when the food trolley was wheeled into the Play Room. In the course of time I became her regular feeder. One day, coming home from town later than we had intended, Ena and I found that all the kids had been fed and wheeled into their bedrooms, all—except one. Sze Sze had refused to be fed by any of the other staff members. She was waiting alone in the Play Room, expecting to be fed by me. She showed possessiveness I did not think appropriate.

As I fed her, I tried to decide how to deal with this situation, in a roundabout way or directly. I chose to use a straightforward approach. "Listen, Sze Sze," I began, "I enjoy spending time with you, feeding you—you know that, don't you—and I know you like that too."

She acknowledged my statement.

"Please, don't think Uncle Bill has come all the way from Canada to be Chan Wing Sze's personal attendant." I continued, "Auntie Ena and I are here to spend time with all of the family. If for one reason or other I can't help you with your meal, give someone else that pleasure. Now staff has to wait for you to finish your meal and put you to bed. That's not fair to them, is it?"

Sze Sze looked taken aback.

"Now, don't think I love you less because of this," I said as I wheeled her into her bedroom. "I may not like everything you do, Sze Sze, but I will always love you."

As in other families, meal times became occasions for sharing. I began telling Sze Sze about life in Canada, talking about our family, relating personal experiences, helping her to get to know me better. It was when we were together, however, in the garden or some quiet corner that I learned to communicate with her and got to know *her* better. I had been told: "When the answer to your question is *yes*, she will stick out her tongue; if she holds her tongue, it is *no*." I soon learned, however, it could also mean *I don't know* or *I don't want to talk about it*.

My efficiency in communicating with Sze Sze increased as my ability to read her body language improved. Watching the way she sat or sagged in her chair, observing how tense or relaxed her muscles were, studying her face to gauge her mood and, above all, looking at her eyes. Those mirrors of her soul—betraying how she feels, communicating her desires, questioning my words and asserting her will—helped me better understand what was going on in her heart and mind than anything else.

Spending time with our young friend, talking with her, observing her reactions to what she heard and saw happening around her, convinced me that she is—if not bright—at least of average intelligence. Then I read her file. It came with her when she moved into the home when she was about 9 years old. It stated that she was considered severely physically *and* mentally disabled. This file was made up of an extensive compilation of reports and assessments, the result of many years of tests, examinations and observations by the medical establishment, social service agencies and educational institutions.

Secret Riches, a book telling the story of the Home of Loving Faithfulness, more charitably states, that when Sze Sze settled in at the home, "It quickly became apparent that she was not as severely mentally handicapped as her reports suggested."[7] Neither assessment of Sze Sze, however, deals fairly with her. Those who read her file for professional reasons will treat her as severely mentally deficient, talk about her in her presence, make decisions for or about her without involving her, thinking she will not understand. Those who read the book are left with the impression that she is somewhat mentally challenged. They may treat her as a child or deal with her in a patronizing manner. Both labels—severely or moderately mentally disabled—will stick to her like barnacles to a barge, wherever she goes, for as long as she lives, impacting on how she sees herself.

Many people who see a physically disabled person may assume she is also mentally deficient, an assumption that is reinforced when she is unable to respond verbally. They don't realize her inability to answer may be a consequence of her physical, not her mental condition. It is disheartening to watch well-meaning visitors to the home make this mistake. After entertaining the family with simple stories or songs, they mix with them, playing games, handing out presents or offering prayers for them. Some approach Sze Sze, speak patronizingly to her and mumble a prayer. They pray without asking if she wants it or knowing what her needs are. They retreat uncomfortably when she directs a quizzical look at them and move quickly to the next wheelchair. Assuring visitors Sze Sze understands both English and Cantonese perfectly, showing them how to communicate with her, and hoping they will make the effort to talk with her, is often futile. Because they feel uncomfortable in the presence of someone who is different, they won't even try. It is difficult to calculate the cumulative damage such repeatedly demeaning treatment does to her spirit. It is also truly amazing that, despite being treated so condescendingly, her self-image is as positive as it is.

Sze Sze, My Daughter

I have tried to put myself in Sze Sze's position; I have attempted to sense what she must feel. I couldn't. I therefore decided to do what I could do: determine my attitude toward and treatment of her. During one of our chats I said, "Sze Sze, I think we will be spending a lot of time together when Auntie Ena and I are in Hong Kong. I'm sure you will like that."

A smile spread across her face.

"Well, my friend, I've tried to put myself in your shoes to see what life for you is like. I can't imagine what it's like to have others do for me all the things I do without giving them much thought—bathing, brushing my teeth, combing my hair (the little I have), taking a forkful of food to my mouth—so I asked myself, If I were Sze Sze, how would I want others to treat me?"

She looked at me, curiously, possibly wondering what I was up to, perhaps trying to guess what would come next.

After a brief pause, I continued, "I will respect you like I would any able-bodied person. I realize you are physically handicapped, but I feel there is nothing wrong with your mind. I will talk with you as I do with Auntie Ena or Auntie Val. I know you can't answer me back like they can, but you can show whether or not you agree with what I say, can't you? Don't be afraid to disagree. Just because I'm older than you doesn't mean I'm always right or know everything. I have been wrong before, and I'm sure there will be times I will be again. Do you understand what I am saying?"

Her smile told me she did.

"I also promise not to make any decisions for you," I went on. "When you make a choice, I will respect it, even if I disagree with it. I may or may not tell you what I would have chosen, but I will not twist your arm to make you change your mind. I will be honest with you, and I trust you to be true with me."

She watched me closely and listened with intense interest.

I waited before I went on, giving her time to digest what I had said. Then I continued, "The only way for me to know what you are thinking is to ask questions. Now, if it ever happens that I ask a question I have no right to ask—there are things you may not want to discuss with me or anyone else—you have the right, like all other people, to keep your thoughts to yourself. Do you think you can live with this?"

I waited for her tongue to come out. It didn't. When Sze Sze is excited or emotional, she finds it difficult to do so. I did see her eyes, locked into mine, slowly filling with tears.

I gave her time to compose herself. When she began to smile, I asked, "Are you telling me this is how we will treat each other, with trust and respect?"

This time she brought out her tongue as far as she could.

I do not know if anyone had ever talked to her in this way or treated her in this manner, but I do know this: Our mutual understanding of how we should deal with each other laid the foundation for our friendship. Acting upon it consistently cemented it.

One of my responsibilities, besides doing a variety of maintenance jobs, was supervising Nicholas Tse. Nick, a Hong Kong pop icon, the naughty boy of the Hong Kong pop scene (an image, I believe, created for him by the media and those who managed his career), had been sentenced to do community service for leaving the scene of a single car accident. Part of that sentence he would serve in the Home of Loving Faithfulness. I had been asked to coordinate and supervise his work at the home. Whatever his reputation in the world of pop culture, at the home he proved to be a young man with Job-like patience, great carefulness and tender compassion, spending endless hours teaching Anna how to strum her guitar, playing with Emmanuel in the pool and helping Tung Tung explore her world.

While I was busy with my maintenance and supervisory work, there was one problem I kept mulling over and over: What can I do to improve communication with Sze Sze? When I initiated a conversation, which was most of the time—people with her condition are passive communicators—we didn't have much trouble talking. There were times, however, usually when she wanted to tell me something, that we ran into difficulties. Sze Sze has ways of showing she wants to share, a sudden movement and a certain look. At other times she seems preoccupied with something, and I will ask if there is anything she wants to get off her mind.

One day she looked rather pensive. I had a feeling she wanted to share something with me and asked, "Is there something you want to tell me?"

Yes.

"About how you feel?"

No.

"About something that has happened?"

Yes.

"At the home?"

No.

"The center?"
No.
"To someone in your family?"
Yes.
"Mother?"
No.
"Brother?"
A hesitant yes.
"The one who visited with his wife last month?"
No.

I looked at her, puzzled. I had been told she had only one brother. It took many more questions before I was able to find out about another brother, a younger one who had died in his teens.

There were times I felt like giving up in frustration, but I suspected that her vexation (trying to tell what was on her heart) was considerably greater than mine (attempting to dig it out of her.) Therefore I would tell her, "You know what, Sze Sze, I'm a bit dense today, but I do want to know what you are trying to tell me. Let it rest. Later I'll try again." I always did. I wanted her to know that what she tried to tell me was important to me. At no time did I leave any of her stories untold. I could afford to take the time to listen. I had something others in the home didn't have: the luxury of time—time to wait, to think, to guess, to uncover what she wanted me to know. Of necessity, communication between staff and Sze Sze is often a one-way street. Care givers will tell what is expected of her, let her know what they will do to or for her or, perhaps, find out a preference, but they lack the advantage of spending quality time with her because there are twenty-plus other members of the family waiting for their attention. There are no such restraints on Ena's and my time.

When communication bogged down, two questions often came to mind: What is it like for Sze Sze to be prisoner of her body, unable to let others know what lives inside her, helpless to share things that are important to her, and powerless to defend herself when wronged? The second question, naturally arising from the first one, was: What can I do to break or bend back the bars that hold her hostage and pry open the doors of her prison? That first question was poignantly answered in a poem Sze Sze loved a lot but one she seldom asked me to read. It described too painfully her condition.

I know what the caged bird feels, alas!
When the sun is bright on the upland slopes;

Sze Sze, My Daughter

When the wind stirs soft through the springing grass
And the river flows like a stream of glass;
When the first bird sings and the first bud opes,
And the faint perfume from its chalice steals –
I know what the caged bird feels!

I know why the caged bird beats its wing
Till its blood is red on the cruel bars;
For he must fly back to his perch and cling
When he fain would be on the bough a-swing;
And a pain still throbs in the old, old scars
And they pulse again with a keener sting –
I know why he beats his wing!

I know why the caged bird sings, ah me,
When his wing is bruised and his bosom sore –
When he beats his bars and would be free;
It is not a carol of joy or glee,
But a prayer that he sends from his heart's deep core,
A plea, that upward to Heaven he flings –
I know why the caged bird sings.[8]

The first time I recited that poem, she listened, hanging on every word. Tears filled her eyes, telling me she is that bird. A thousand thoughts—thoughts to be shared, challenged and tested, thoughts unable to soar, thoughts broken on the cruel bars of a dysfunctional body—are caged in her mind. When she does try to share them, she lacks the physical ability and language proficiency to express them. Her listeners often lack the time or patience to dig them out.

Breaking the bars of Sze Sze's prison became an obsession for me, a preoccupation keeping me busy for years to come. She had a communication chart pasted on the tray of her wheelchair, but poor motor skills kept her from using it effectively. Inaccurate pointing often forced me to guess which letter she tried to target, and uncooperative muscles slowed her down. The time and accuracy problems could have been solved if she had allowed me to scan for the letters of the words she wanted to spell, having me point first at the rows and then at the columns on her chart to find which letters she had in mind. She insisted on pointing. I respected her desire to be as independent as possible.

Sze Sze, My Daughter

The nurse in residence assured me that our young friend had learned to read both Chinese and English, but Sze Sze's attempts to use her communication board made me question what I had been told about her English language education. It wasn't her ability to understand spoken English I doubted; I questioned her competence to read or spell it. Her responses to questions about vowels and consonants frequently drew blank stares. When I expressed my doubts to the nurse, she handed me Sze Sze's file and school books. They revealed that her formal English instruction was rudimentary at best.

There was one bit of information in her file, however, that intrigued me. I discovered an assessment, a document stating she should be able to access a computer, a positive report from the Hong Kong Polytechnic University that had gathered dust for three years. My request to the Aunties to reactivate her file, to have her reassessed, was granted. I had to act quickly because the end of our visit to the home was nearing rapidly and the Chinese New Year was approaching fast. Remembering not to make any decisions for Sze Sze, I asked her that evening at devotion time if she remembered being tested at Polytech.

Yes.

"Would you like me to make an appointment to have you retested? I want to see if you can use a computer."

Sze Sze began to bounce on her mattress, a sure sign she was excited.

"I will phone Polytech tomorrow."

Sze Sze had her initial assessment scheduled for January 22. Kim bused us to the university. In a room showcasing all kinds of prosthetic devices, she was welcomed by Doctor Eric and his assistant. They led her through a rigorous program of tests, prodding and pushing her to perform. They made her activate a variety of switches and measured times of response. After working with her for more than an hour, they agreed that she, using the middle finger of her left hand, should be able to access a computer equipped with a special peripheral. A second appointment was made for four o'clock on January 30, the last workday of the year on the Chinese calendar.

On our second visit, a prosthetics technician strapped a temporary splint to Sze Sze's left arm, keeping it from moving aimlessly. He secured all fingers but the middle one with Velcro straps and fastened with sticky stuff a micro switch under the tip of that finger. While she did eye-hand coordination exercises, the technician kept making adjustments to the splint. He loosened some straps and tightened others, and he changed the placement of the switch until Doctor Eric was satisfied. The technician then removed the splint and promised to make it a perfect fit for Sze Sze's hand.

After the New Year, Sze Sze would begin with daily, eye-hand coordination exercises using her splint. Its switch would be connected temporarily to a feedback device, and that gadget would eventually be replaced by a computer with an onscreen, scanning keyboard. Doctor Eric was confident our young friend would learn to write using a computer. Because Ena and I would return to Canada soon after the Chinese New Year, I would not be there to help her with exercises, but I hoped she would, with the help of others, be ready to use a computer by the time we returned to Hong Kong.

Traveling back to the home, Sze Sze was both tired and excited. She was exhausted by having been pushed to the limit, challenged to give it her all, and enthusiastic about the prospect of a better way of communication. The assessments and their outcomes marked the beginning of years of raised hopes and promises, challenges and demands, disappointments and frustrations, and eventually . . . .

Chapter 3

The months between our return to Canada and our next departure for Hong Kong were marked by ups and downs. Those highs and lows were propelled by family circumstances and jolted by health concerns, both personal and global, sending our emotions on a rollercoaster ride. Some of our children went through relationship changes. One, after struggling for a number of years in her marriage, began to find stability. Another, after years of emotional abuse, walked away from a wealthy but controlling partner. A third, ending years of substance abuse, found sobriety, peace with God and a god-fearing wife.

A stress tolerance test pointed to possible blockages in one or more of my arteries, and further investigation was scheduled to take place a week after our next return from Hong Kong. A neurologist, after examining Ena, assured her that she does not have Alzheimer's, but left us in the dark about the cause of her memory loss. All these concerns reminded us not to take our health for granted. The outbreak of a new respiratory disease in China rapidly spread to Hong Kong and other parts of the world, including Canada. The infection caused death, turmoil economic disruption and uncertainty. It made us wonder whether or not to travel to Hong Kong at that time.

We decided to wait and see. As soon as the World Health Organization lifted the advisory it had issued against traveling to Hong Kong, we were off again. We set aside the paranoid demands of the board of Serene Meadows Housing Society, bidding us to postpone our trip. They feared we would return infected, carry back with us the deadly SARS virus, infect the residents of our complex and decimate its population.

It was in late May that our JAL flight landed in Hong Kong. It had been a long flight, passing over Vancouver Island, skirting Alaska and the Aleutians and crossing the International Date Line. After we transferred at Narita, our flight followed the spine of Taiwan, approached Lantau Island, and finally touched down on the tarmac at Chek Lap Kok, Hong Kong's international airport, where it slowly taxied to Terminal One.

It was good to be back. I felt confident, well-prepared and eager to begin the work I had planned for the next three months. I was ready to teach Sze Sze reading and spelling and expressing herself better through writing. I was well equipped, I felt, to help our friend liberate herself, bend back the bars of her cage and pry open the gates of her prison.

My laptop was brimming with phonics charts, spelling lessons and reading instructions. My briefcase held WiVik software ready to be installed on Sze Sze's Compaq laptop. That program included an onscreen, scanning keyboard, Word Q, and word expansion features, which made possible the writing of words and phrases with a minimum of keystrokes. With the assistance of modern technology, my many years of experience as special needs teacher and Sze Sze's enthusiasm and courage we were bound to succeed. I was ready to forge new and better ways for our friend to communicate.

I had no illusion that what I hoped to accomplish would be easy. Never before had I taught a student as handicapped as Sze Sze. Both of us, however, were full of confidence, a confidence that gave us courage, a courage that filled us with hope, and hope, St. Paul assures us, doesn't disappoint. I didn't think, at that time, I was overconfident, trying to do the impossible, attempting to construct castles in the air. But even if I were, had not Thoreau convincingly argued that such "work need not be lost. There is where they should be." All I needed to do was put solid foundations under them.[8] Failure was not an option. I was ready to hit the ground running.

It took Uncle Pete, our office manager and resident computer whiz, some time to get WiVik installed and all its features working properly. It took me a few days to figure out how it all worked. It took little time, however, to realize the program was not without quirks, that it had a mind of its own. So did Sze Sze. There were times she viewed her computer as an interesting toy, a plaything rather than a tool to help her learn, when she decided to waste her own as well as the limited time I had to teach her.

Most of the time, though, Sze Sze tried her best, was anxious to please and eager to succeed, but that, too, presented problems. For her to control the switch on her splint successfully, her muscles needed to be relaxed. The moment she tried too hard to push that little red button at the right time, her timing would go awry, pushing too soon, too late or too often. Perseveration, the inability to stop her finger from pushing the switch repeatedly in rapid succession, proved to be a problem. The first activation of the switch brought the desired letter or word to the screen, the second one returned the cursor to its starting position, the next prompted the delete key and wiped out what she had just accomplished.

Even at the best of times, however, I wondered about the placement of the micro switch on the splint. Observing and manipulating the movements of Sze Sze's left middle finger for an hour in the carefully controlled setting of a laboratory at Polytech was one level of reality, the ideal setting in which the splint had been designed. Teaching and encouraging Sze Sze how to use it day after day in the home, a place with many distractions, was a different reality, the real world which put the design to the test, a test it did not pass.

Before Sze Sze could work on her computer, she had to be readied. Her left forearm was strapped to the hard plastic splint, her thumb and all but one finger Velcroed out of the way and her middle finger left free to operate the switch. Under ideal circumstances, when her muscles were fully relaxed, the tip of her outstretched finger would cover the switch, waiting for the right moment to activate it. However, her muscles are weak; they tire easily, making it difficult to repeatedly push the button. Bending her finger at the first joint would give it more push power, but shortened it, making it difficult for her finger to reach the switch. Frustration would set in, causing stress, making even her outstretched finger shrink enough to miss the target.

Had the switch been properly placed, had Sze Sze's muscles been relaxed most of the time and had they been strong and tireless always, would that have solved her problem of accessing her computer? Not likely. To understand what causes her problems, we must remember that when her heart stopped, starving her brain of oxygen, the cerebellum was damaged beyond repair. It is the area of the central nervous system responsible for processing signals, impulses from other parts of the brain to the muscles, enabling smooth and coordinated movements.

Now try to imagine Sze Sze at her computer. She has been strapped to her splint. Her left middle finger is ready to push the little, red button. She is trying to write the word *therefore*. Having successful typed *th*—prompting the words *than*, *that*, *the*, *then*, *there*, *therefore* and *this* to appear in the Word Q to the left of her scanning keyboard—she now intently eyes the scanner. It highlights, one at a time, the words in the Word Q. It slowly scans down the list, pauses a few seconds at every word and approaches the desired word. Finally, *therefore* is highlighted. Her brain sends the message *push* to her left middle finger. The signal races along neurons and synapses to the cerebellum and expects to be processed, coordinated and passed on to the finger. Instead it is sabotaged, scrambled, delayed, ignored, repeated or sidetracked. As a result, the wrong word or no word at all appears on the screen, or whatever word does appear is immediately deleted.

Sze Sze had her good and not-so-good days. The good ones gave us courage and hope, the not-so-good ones discouragement and frustration, more to me, although I tried not to show it, than to Sze Sze. Living most of her life with serious disabilities had given her a remarkably high threshold for frustration. She could struggle with her switch for a quarter of an hour, putting two or three words on the screen, deleting them in a second's time, starting all over again and seldom showing any signs of anger or frustration. When fatigue or frustration did begin to show, I shut down the computer or told her a story of some disabled person who had succeeded despite serious handicaps. Sometimes we played a game or went for a walk in the garden. She needed little encouragement to bounce back to her courageous self.

The not-so-good days outnumbered the good ones, it seemed. It soon became clear not to rely too heavily on modern technology or bank too much on the computer as a tool to help break down barriers to communication. Of course, working on the computer made up only a small part of the time I spent teaching Sze Sze. Sessions on the computer lasted seldom more than one half hour. Those periods were quite intense, demanded much of her concentration and sapped a great deal of her energy. Any time spent on the computer beyond those thirty minutes often proved counterproductive. I spent, therefore, considerable time and effort on other things: the teaching of reading and spelling. Both needed much work.

Those computer lessons were useful in more than one way; they exposed more than physical roadblocks. They revealed that accessibility of the computer was only one problem facing us. As I watched Sze Sze—studying words that appeared on Word Q and trying to choose the correct one—I observed she was often hesitant and not always sure of her choices. Sometimes she allowed the desired word to be highlighted more than once and let it pass repeatedly. Finally, she would look at me and question me with her eyes. I realized there was a lot of work waiting for me. If she struggled in reading, the passive area of language arts, I knew I would have my work cut out in spelling, the constructive part. It confirmed my earlier suspicion that her formal instruction in English left much to be desired.

I assumed, therefore, Sze Sze had no formal English education at all and decided to start my language instruction at the very beginning, combining reading and spelling and relying heavily on phonics. I first taught her the short vowel sounds. I then encouraged her to form simple words by combining those sounds with consonants having a single sound. Next I asked her to spell on the computer the words she had learned to read. For whatever reason—the shortness of the words, their familiarity, good visual memory or just plain luck, she did remarkably well . . . at first.

When more sounds were added, however, she began to falter. A simple test revealed what I feared: a difficulty in discriminating between short vowel sounds. She was able to distinguish between those sounds when pronounced in isolation, but she became confused when they were tucked between consonant sounds. She was doing relatively well as long as I taught her words just having short *a* sounds, as in *bat* and *hat*, but she was no longer sure of herself when short *e* sounds were added to the mix, as in *bat* and *bet*. She was lost when, in addition, she had to distinguish those sounds from short *i* sounds, as in *pat*, *pet* and *pit,* and short *o* and *u* sounds, as in *hat*, *hit*, *hot* and *hut*. The addition of long vowel sounds completed her confusion. All this made me suspect Sze Sze might have a learning disability.

Teaching Sze Sze to read presented me with a new challenge: never before had I taught a student who was unable to vocalize. I had to devise checks to make sure that she was reading the words I had taught, that she actually read what I thought or hoped she was reading.

Being unable to speak also posed a problem for my student, a difficulty that may well have caused all or part of her inability to discriminate between similar sounds. Because she was unable to imitate the sounds I modeled for her, Sze Sze found it difficult to distinguish between them. There is, I believe, a close connection between the feel, the resonance, of the sounds we produce and those we hear. Each sound creates its own peculiar range of vibrations and reaches our ears by two pathways: one internal, through our facial bones, and the other external, via the airwaves. I had observed earlier that some of my special needs students, those who had speech impairments and needed therapy, often had difficulties spelling correctly the words they found hard to pronounce. I began to realize we would be in for an uphill battle, but together we soldiered on, bravely, rejoicing in small victories, dealing with failures the best we could.

By now it had become clear that the marvels of modern technology—computers adapted to the needs of the disabled and software expressly designed for their use—wonderful as they are, have their limitations. It was also becoming obvious that my expertise as special needs teacher was seriously challenged, that my methods needed rethinking and that my approaches called for different ideas. All this made me wonder if I had bitten off more than I could chew. Considering that two of the three supports on which I thought our success would rest—the help of technology and my experience as teacher—had, if not knocked out from under us, suffered severe blows, we were left with the least dependable pillar on which we hoped to construct the castle of our success: Sze Sze's enthusiasm and courage.

To depend on the enthusiasm and courage of an able-bodied person is one thing; to bank on the exuberance and confidence of someone with multiple handicaps is an entirely different story. It is true, I have often been amazed at Sze Sze's ability to bounce back from serious setbacks and inspired by her capacity to recover from daunting disappointments. However, I have also been shaken by her periods of sadness and moments of hopelessness. Those dark moods were caused not by her unsuccessful struggles to access a computer, her inability to spell certain words or her failure to distinguish between different vowel sounds. They were brought on by the realization of the deep loss resulting from her disability. The impairment had stolen her childhood—that carefree time of romping with other children, playing on swings and splashing barefoot in wading pools. Her handicap had robbed her of her youth—that wonderfully magic time of forming special friendships, sharing secrets with soul mates and making plans for the future. She knew her future would never hold a university education, a career, a lover, a husband or a child.

One morning, on entering the Play Room, I found Sze Sze slumped in her chair. The radiant smile, her usual morning greeting, was absent; the light in her eyes, always so expressive, had gone out and sadness had taken its place. I pulled up a stool, sat beside her and began, "Morning, Sze Sze, things are not so good this morning, are they—had a run in with one of the staff?"

No reply.

"Are you in pain?"
No.
"Angry . . . unhappy . . . sad . . .?"
She slowly stuck out her tongue.
"Did anything happen at the center to make you sad?"
No.

Earlier she had told me about a resident at the center, a young man, wheelchair bound and, like her, unable to speak, someone she liked. He had started to ignore her, causing her to be both angry and sad. It had taken her some time to get over it.

"Do you feel lonely?" Tears slowly began to fill her eyes and course down her cheeks.

It is possible to feel lonely in a crowd, nameless in a multitude and unknown in a throng. It is equally conceivable to live in a home with twenty-plus other family members, receive care from an attentive staff, attend a day center crowded with others like yourself and feel alone, isolated and separated from the real world. Sze Sze felt that way. What she needed were other teens to befriend her, to talk about things that interest young people, to share secrets and longings and to giggle about silly things. No matter how much she liked me as a teacher or trusted me as a friend, I could never fill the social void she felt—after all, I was old enough to be her grandfather. From that time on I began to pray for a young person to volunteer at the home, someone who could be to her what I could never be—a sister and confidante, someone with whom she could feel what she was meant to be: a carefree teenager.

During our spring visit in 2003, Sze Sze's wheelchair was in need of a major overhaul. This robbed her of its use for about two weeks and forced her to use one of Fu Fu's old chairs. That chair lacked the straps needed to hold her in a secure position, stripped her of the use of her neck brace, deprived her of the tray and its support posts and left her sagging in obvious discomfort. Just one look at her was enough to see how uncomfortable she was. Because she was not secure in Fu Fu's chair, she was not allowed to go to the center.

One day, when I came to collect Sze Sze for her lessons, she lay crumpled in Fu Fu's chair, misery written all over her face. When I asked her what made her look so glum, one of the care givers piped up, "Oh, she is selfish again, she wants her own wheelchair. Fu Fu's isn't good enough for her. I told her to think about all the disabled children in Third World countries who have no chair at all." This remark was foolish and insensitive. All she saw in Sze Sze was a job, not a person; all she noticed was sadness, not the suffering which caused it. Neither did she notice the angry glare Sze Sze shot at her, her only self-defense.

This incident made me wonder what it feels like when you hear yourself maligned, what goes through your mind when you are falsely accused, and what emotions are aroused when you are slandered and cannot speak up for yourself or clear your name. Utter impotence! How often has this happened to Sze Sze and others like her?

We also had fun times. Sze Sze loves to play games. One of the games she learned to play was SKIP BO. Winning at cards depends as much on the hand that you are dealt as on how you play it. She soon proved to be a card shark. She carefully surveyed the cards exposed on the table and shrewdly played the cards I held for her. Sometimes she passed—even when I thought she should have played—often she proved to be correct in her decisions and frequently won. She caught on equally quickly with checkers and other strategy games.

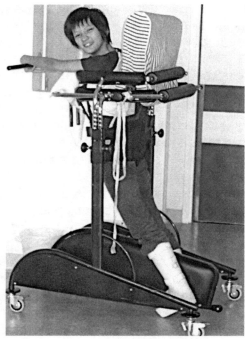

Sze Sze in her walker

This was also the time she learned to walk using Tak Tak's walking frame. For the first time in her life she was on her feet, moved freely from place to place and decided for herself where to go or whether to go. It gave her a sense of freedom she had never before experienced. Never before had she possessed the liberty to explore places, examine every corner of the communal dining room, roam through the living room of the Lower Ark, stand in front of the kitchen window or make it to the garden on her own feet. It was an activity that took much of her energy. It also was an exercise that gave her a feeling of self-determination and filled her with great joy.

Chapter 4

The family is well-cared for. Every morning while the kids are bathed, beds are stripped, bed frames and mattresses are wiped clean, freshly laundered linens are put on beds and clothes from individual wardrobes are laid out. Everyone is fresh at all times; there never is an institutional smell anywhere. The physical care of the family is second to none. Yet, Ena and I felt something was lacking.

It took us some time to put our finger on that *something*, but one day, after the family had been fed their lunch and put to bed for a nap, and care givers began to drift to the staff dining room, it came to me. Some of the staff helped Ah Ying, our cook, by putting the dishes she had prepared on the tables; others found a place at one of two tables, Cantonese speakers around one, English and bilingual speakers, mostly Westerners and Filipinos, around the other. When the long hand of the clock approached twelve, the chatter and banter died down, and some at the Chinese table turned to see who at the bilingual table would say grace. Then it hit me. It struck me as peculiar. None of the staff—most of whom are not Christians, care little whether or by whom their food is blessed and likely regard *amen* as the signal to dig in—will eat a bite until someone has blessed their food. Strange, because no one pauses to do the same for those who are cared for in the home, members of a Christian family. When the food trolley is wheeled into the Play Room, care givers collect the food for the persons they will feed and, without further ado, start feeding.

When I discussed this oddity with Ena, we discovered a similar lack of spiritual nurture in bedtime routines. Therefore we began to say short prayers for those whom we fed. We also started to do devotions with the family in the evening, stopping at every bed, praying with them and wishing them a good night. Later we expanded our ministry by reading simple Bible stories to those who could understand.

It was while doing evening devotions with Sze Sze that I got to know another side of her. I discovered a different dimension of her character: I saw a soul with a sincere love for her Lord; I witnessed a heart eager to follow her Savior; I found a mind hungry to know him more deeply; I uncovered struggles, questions and doubts similar to those of other believers; and I observed a faith tested, at times severely, but never wasted by the hardships brought upon her by her disabilities.

One evening I asked Sze Sze if she had been baptized. Her response was a puzzled look, making me wonder if she was ignorant of the sacrament and its significance, or if she did not know the meaning of the word. It turned out *baptize* and *baptism* were not part of her English vocabulary. Once she understood my question, she became quite animated, bouncing all over her mattress. "Are you telling me that you have been baptized?" I asked.

No.

"Oh, you want to receive baptism!"

By now she was so excited that she could barely bring out her tongue. I promised to discuss with the Aunties her desire to receive baptism and make the necessary arrangements. The Aunties made no objections, and Pastor Cui of Breakthrough Ministries agreed to baptize Sze Sze on the afternoon of Saturday, August 23, two days before our return to Canada.

Two and a half weeks, that was all the time we had to get ready for the great event. Sze Sze and I agreed it would be good to review what it means to be a Christian. She wanted to refresh what she knew about the teachings to which she as a believer should assent, embrace as true and essential, and believe with all her heart. We would use a simplified catechism I had put together for a Sudanese refugee in our home church. It was a set of lessons based on the *Apostles' Creed*, a confession that succinctly summarizes the basic teachings of our Christian faith.

Sze Sze insisted on choosing the hymns and choruses to be sung at the baptismal service, the speaker who would deliver the message and the passage on which he should speak. Her choice of the place and manner of baptism, immersion, posed a bit of a problem for her. She wanted the baptism to take place in the Breakthrough Chapel, but since it doesn't have a baptismal basin, she had to settle for the swimming pool at the home.

At times Sze Sze has a way of amazing me. She certainly did with the choice of the Scripture passage on which she wanted me to speak. She vetoed all the stories dealing with baptism I showed her: Jesus' baptism by John, the Ethiopian eunuch's by Phillip, the baptisms of Paul, Cornelius, Lydia and the jailer at Philippi—all were rejected. I told her I knew of only one other passage dealing with baptism, and I read to her the first few verses of Romans 6. Her face lit up. That was the passage she had in mind. I wondered where she had heard about it. She seldom goes to church, and she could not have read it for herself, for she is unable to handle a Bible or any other book. It was one of those pleasant surprises she sometimes had for me.

Our time of preparation—the reviewing of those teachings we as Christians believe as true and hold dear—was precious, sometimes emotional and certainly revealing. It brought out some of the issues stirring Sze Sze's heart and mind. When we discussed *"I believe in God the Father, Almighty, Creator of heaven and earth,"* she could wholeheartedly assent to the fact that He is Creator, that He upholds his creation and that He provides for his creatures. However, when I asked her if she believed that He is a loving Father, that He can be trusted that whatever He sends our way, good or bad, He will ultimately turn to our good, her tongue was slow in coming out. When it did, she was weeping.

How difficult it was for this young woman, in the prime of her life—or what should have been—to see the hand of a loving Father in assigning to her the role of spectator, to watch from her wheelchair the world go by, to be unable to take part in its affairs and to know she would be sidelined . . . always. How perplexing it was for her to understand why God, if He truly is her loving Father, would allow her to suffer, not just for a season, but lifelong, and how any good could come from all this suffering.

Her understanding of God as Father was colored by her relationship—or lack of it—with her earthly father. He had left her mother and the family for another woman. After Sze Sze had moved to the Home of Loving Faithfulness, he had visited her a few times and then disappeared from her life. She felt abandoned. Bitter. She didn't mind me talking about her mother or brother and his family, but she resented me mentioning her father, and she could not think of me as a substitute taking his place.

The lesson on *"I believe . . . the forgiveness of sins"* was equally emotional and revealing. When I asked her, "Are you a sinner, do you need to be forgiven?" she acknowledged herself to be a sinner in need of forgiveness. Of course.

Because I dare to be vulnerable with Sze Sze, she feels that her thoughts are safe with me. I decided to open up on this occasion. "You know, Sze Sze," I began, "I may look like a respectable, elderly gentleman, one who would never do anything shocking or criminal, but there are times that I am grateful my thoughts are not projected on a giant television screen, visible to all who pass by. If they were, I would hide myself in shame. What I seem to be on the outside is one thing. Who I am, on the inside, the real me, is, at times, someone entirely different." I looked at her and asked, "Do you ever have thoughts of which you are ashamed?"

A hesitant yes.

For a moment, I felt she wanted to say more, but I wasn't sure. I did not want to embarrass her by prying into her private thoughts, digging for those things she would not want me to know and finding out what would cause her to feel ashamed. Therefore we talked about hidden sins in general. We concluded our lesson with a time of prayer. I then asked what she wanted to do next, work on the computer . . . a spelling lesson . . . go to the garden . . . ?

No. She looked at me, seriously, and swung her hand to the communication board on her tray.

"You want to tell me something . . . something we've talked about . . . hidden sins?"

Yes, and she pointed at *w*.

"When . . . where . . . what . . . ?"

Yes. Next her hand slid to *i*.

"You mean yourself . . . Sze Sze?"

Yes.

"What I . . ."

F

"Find . . . feel . . . ?"

Yes.

"What I feel . . . ?"

Yes. Then she pointed to *y*.

"You . . . ?"

Yes.

"What I feel you . . . ?"

Yes. Her hand stopped moving, and she looked at me with her dark, brown eyes. "Hmm—I think there is a little word missing. Are you trying to say, What I feel *for* you?"

Yes.

"What do you feel for me, Sze Sze?"

Her hand slowly slid to *I*.

"Love?"

Yes. This admission gave me an opportunity to deal with a problem both Ena and I had seen coming. Only a few days earlier, Ena had remarked about the look of adoration in Sze Sze's eyes when she looked at me. I, too, had recognized the look a teacher gets from time to time when one of his teenaged students has a crush on him.

I said to her, "That's wonderful, Sze Sze! I feel the same about you, but . . . you know . . . love is such an overused word. People will say, I *love* your dress, I *love* ice cream or I *love* swimming. What they really mean to say is that they *like* your dress, they *savor* ice cream and they *enjoy* swimming. Do you understand what I mean?"

Yes.

"Besides, there are different kinds of love. Love for friends is a wonderful thing, but the love I have for my children and grandchildren goes deeper. Then there is a very special love, the love a man has for his wife and a wife has for her husband. But the deepest kind of love of all is the love God has for sinners."

I let this sink in for a while, watching carefully for her reaction.

"Sometimes I find it hard to determine what kind of love I feel for you . . . the love for a very dear friend or the love for a daughter . . . I guess either is fine. I can share either kind of love with one or many friends or children." She looked at me fixedly as I spoke, her dark, expressive eyes almost pulling the words from my lips. I went on, "But that third kind of love, that very special love, I may share with only one person. That person is Ena . . . you understand that, don't you?"

With difficulty she stuck out her tongue, and tears began to course down her cheeks. I watched her, slumped in her chair, weeping softly. My heart flooded with a mix of emotions: admiration for her honesty and courage; sadness because my dear friend would never have a special person with whom to share her life and never know the joy of conjugal love; confusion about the seeming injustice of it all.

What Sze Sze had just told me was not so much a profession of what she felt for me as—in the context of our lesson on forgiveness and hidden sins—a confession of the inappropriateness of that affection. It was also an expression of her futile longing to satisfy those feelings all teens experience, urges aroused by hormones coursing through their veins, a visceral awakening, preparing their bodies for pleasure and procreation. It was a cry of hopelessness, moved by the knowledge that for her those desires would never be satisfied.

Would I have had the courage, like she had, to confess sins hidden in the recesses of my heart. It is so much easier to pick up stones to cast at a sinner . . . until we are reminded of Jesus' words that whoever is without sin cast the first one.

This incident made me aware of the danger of two people—one a young woman, though severely physically disabled, yet possessing a magnetic personality and considerable charm, the other an aging gent, well past his prime—working in close physical and emotional proximity. There is the risk that she mistakes the intense attention generated in the one-on-one teaching setting for more than it is meant to be. There is the hazard she misinterprets the affection he feels for her as a friend as a deeper kind of love. There is the potential that he, moved by her physical condition, tries to make up for that of which she has been deprived and attempts to compensate for that which can never be hers. There is the possibility that he, flattered by the adoration of this young woman, becomes infatuated with her. There is the peril of simply giving in to temptation and taking advantage of her. It gave me reason for serious reflection.

After we had composed ourselves, and I had cleaned up Sze Sze's face, I got ready to bring her to the Play Room to be fed, but again she indicated she wanted to tell me something and pointed to *j* on her board.

"Jesus . . .?"

Yes, and she moved her finger to *s*.

"Sin . . . Sze Sze . . .?"

Yes.

"Jesus Sze Sze . . . ."

F.

"Feel . . . find . . . friend . . .?"

Yes.

"Oh, you are telling me that Jesus is Sze Sze's friend," I ventured. "Of course he is!"

No.

"*Is* Jesus Sze Sze's friend?" I asked. "Do you want to know if Jesus will *still* be Sze Sze's friend? Certainly! I'm sure he is! He will always be! You believe that when you confess your sins, he will forgive them, don't you?"

Yes.

There was a smile of relief on Sze Sze's face when I wheeled her into the Play Room for tea.[10]

Our final lesson was on "*I believe . . . the resurrection of the body, and the life everlasting.*" This was a lesson that gave Sze Sze intense joy. Just to think there will come a time that she will be in the presence of Jesus, when she will have a body that will allow her to do all the things she can't do in her disabled state—walk and dance, speak and sing, dress and groom herself—filled her with unspeakable joy that radiated from her face. For us able-bodied people, the idea of being without sniffles, painful bunions and arthritic joints is something to which we look forward. For those who live all their lives with multiple handicaps, who totally depend on others for bathing and dressing, grooming and feeding, the idea of being able to do all those things themselves must be something otherworldly, something for which they long with great anticipation.

After we had concluded our lesson, I asked if she wanted to go for a walk. Yes, later. She first wanted to tell me something. With the help of her board she told me "I don't want help," and then rolled up her eyes. I said, "I don't understand . . . What is it you are trying to tell me?" Then it dawned on me. I laughed, "Are you telling me you don't want any help in heaven?"

Yes.

I assured her once more that in heaven she would not need any help. Her face radiated joy.

Our three-month visit to the home was quickly coming to an end, and there was still much work to be done before we could board our plane for the journey home: maintenance and building projects waited to be completed, tasks for Nick were to be organized and supervised, lessons for Sze Sze had to be planned and taught, final preparations for the baptismal service had to be made and Sze Sze needed to be encouraged.

As we came closer to the end of our visit, Sze Sze began to show signs of discouragement. After a particularly depressing day, I sat down with her to get at the bottom of her dejection. She told me she was disappointed that, after three months of hard work, she was not yet able to read and write English.

"Let's put what we've done in perspective," I said. "Do you think you are Superwoman?"

She shot me a puzzled look.

"Listen carefully to what I'm going to say, my friend," I continued. "Do you have any idea how long it takes a child of average intelligence—one who does not have any disabilities and is born and raised in a country where everyone speaks English—to learn reading, spelling, basic grammar and writing? It will take her six hours a day, five days a week, nine months a year for three years. You've done well, but there is much more to be done. You can't compare yourself with an average Canadian child. English isn't your first language, you have multiple handicaps and you have been learning to read and write for only three months. Perhaps you are expecting a bit too much of yourself—and of me. If, after such a short time, you would be able to read and write, you would be Superwoman. Do you understand what I'm saying?"

She smiled a weak yes.

"There's a lot of hard work waiting for both of us. There will be times of success but also moments of discouragement. We are only at the beginning. We've spent only three months on this project. Now is a good time to determine if it will all be worth the effort; now is the time to make up your mind if you want to continue or throw in the towel. I will abide by whatever you decide. Do you want some time to think over what I've said?"

She looked at me as if to say, Are you kidding!

"Your eyes tell me you are not a quitter. We will need a lot of help in what we are trying to accomplish, Sze Sze. Do you know what it says in Philippians 4:13?"

No.

"I can do everything through him who gives me strength." I'm sure you know who it is that gives strength—right!"

Her smile told me she did. At that point, Auntie Wendy, who had come in and had been listening in on part of our conversation, said, "I suggest you add to this 2 Corinthians 12:10, 'For when I am weak, then I am strong.'"

Saturday August 23 was a busy day at the Home of Loving Faithfulness. After breakfast, Ena went straight to the kitchen in the Lower Ark to bake apricot bars and other delicacies. I disappeared into the main kitchen to make *oliebollen*, Dutch fruit fritters, at Sze Sze's request. Staff cleared the Play Room of unused wheelchairs and other unwanted items, placed rows of chairs for the invited guests and made sure to leave the best places for those who were in wheelchairs. Still others readied the dining room, preparing it for the reception which would follow the baptismal service. The home became a beehive of unusual activities.

In the afternoon, guests began to arrive. The family members were wheeled into the Play Room, soon to be joined by a throng of people, Sze Sze's friends. She had told me that she has many friends, but it wasn't until that day I realized how many. Besides her mother, there were teachers and former students of Elaine Field School, a school for spastic children she had attended. They were soon joined by recovering addicts from St. Stephen's Society, Jackie Pullinger's drug rehabilitation institution, regular visitors to the home. Of course, residents of Wah Sum Centre, a home for spastic adults, an institution Sze Sze attended as day client five days a week, were not missing. Volunteers and friends of the home came drifting in. The presence of all who showed up was a testimony to the popularity of this young woman, an affirmation of the force and attraction of her character.

After the buzz of friends exchanging greetings had died down, the wheelchair-bound guests had been wriggled into place and their escorts had found places to sit, Auntie Wendy spoke some words of welcome and opened with prayer. We sang a few hymns and choruses, and I was given the opportunity to present my message, which was translated by Pui Yee. Keeping in mind my audience—a mix of Christians and people to whom the teachings of Christianity and its rituals were foreign—I presented a short explanation of the symbolism of baptism. I also gave the reason why it was important to Sze Sze to receive this sacrament: to testify of her love for Christ and his redeeming love for her. The service was concluded with her favorite chorus, *Give Thanks with a Grateful Heart*.

Then Sze Sze was whisked off to her bedroom to change into a baptismal gown. From there she was wheeled to the pool side, where Pastor Cui, Ah Lam and I were waiting in our gowns to receive her. Because Sze Sze was very excited, we expected her involuntary movements to be excessive. Therefore we had asked Ah Lam, an evangelist and friend of the home, to assist. Flanked by Ah Lam and me, her face radiant and her left leg locked firmly between mine to keep her upright, Sze Sze answered the pastor's questions with confidence. Then came the immersion. It was a triumphant Sze Sze who emerged, right hand raised high.

Sze Sze, My Daughter

Sze Sze's baptism

By the time we got back into dry clothes, the guests had moved to the dining room, digging into refreshments that had been prepared by volunteers, staff and caterers, a true smorgasbord. Sze Sze was in the thick of it, surrounded by friends, sampling delicacies and basking in the attention. That evening, when we made the rounds in the bedrooms, we found waiting for us a tired young woman, her joy tinged with a touch of sadness, Uncle Bill and Auntie Ena would be leaving for Canada in two days.

That last Sunday passed quickly. The bright, sunny weather of the day before had given way to strong winds and pelting rain. The number three storm signal was up, a typhoon was brushing by Hong Kong. We said goodbye to the kids at devotion time. I pulled up a stool beside Sze Sze's bed and sat beside her. After devotions, we talked about her studies. A number of people had volunteered to work with her while we were away. I encouraged her to work hard at her computer skills, spelling and reading. Then we prayed. It was hard to say goodbye. Sze Sze was becoming very precious to me.

The following morning the number three signal was still in effect. It meant that none of the family would be going to school or center. They were still in bed when we were about to leave. We had one more opportunity to see them. I went to see Sze Sze, lowered the bedrail and sat beside her, my arm resting on the edge of her mattress. Lying on her tummy, as she usually does, she placed her cheek on my arm. When I said goodbye to her once more, she pushed herself up, opened her mouth wide, and gently dug her teeth into my cheek.

Chapter 5

In the car park we hugged our friends who saw us off, the Aunties, Pui Yee and Uncle Pete and Auntie Sue, and we promised to be back early in the next year. Kim had already loaded our suitcases into the van and was waiting for us. On the highway we could feel the wind shake our vehicle, and I wondered aloud if airplanes would be flying in weather like this. "Don't worry, Bill," Kim assured us, "we're used to this kind of weather in Hong Kong. No planes will be grounded when the number three signal is in effect." He was right, at the airport it was business as usual, and we departed on time.

During the first part of our trip, we experienced so much turbulence, even the cabin crew was commanded to remain seated. It augured the tempestuous reception we would encounter upon our arrival at Serene Meadows. In June we had received an e-mail from the board of our housing society demanding that we, upon arrival in Canada, go into quarantine for ten days at a location other than our condominium. Our response to this absurd and unreasonable demand had been that we, as we had promised before we left for Hong Kong, would follow the rules issued by the Fraser Health Authority. We also informed the board that two weeks earlier the World Health Organization had declared Hong Kong to be free of SARS and that our return to Canada was still two months away. Therefore there would be no danger of us infecting the residents of our community, and going into quarantine would be unnecessary.

It was early afternoon when we arrived at Serene Meadows. We were tired, eager to unpack our suitcases and more than ready to get rested, but we were unable to enter our apartment. Before we left for Hong Kong, the board had informed us that, because of recent break-ins, deadbolt locks would be installed on the doors of all apartments. They had asked us permission to enter our home to have the work done during our absence. We had told them that we had no objections to them doing the work while we were gone. Because we had not yet received the key to this new lock, we went in search of Maximilian Fast, the president of the board. He was nowhere to be found.

Max was a man much aware of his own importance. The strut in his stride demonstrated the numerous responsibilities resting on his shoulders, and the authority injected into his gravelly voice spoke eloquently of the gravity of his office. Perhaps, because of his prestigious position in our small community, he thought of himself a bit more highly than he should have. It is also possible that he was not always as well-informed as he imagined himself to be. To be sure, he was cognizant of all that happened at Serene Meadows, but his awareness of what was going on in the world beyond his domain was, at times, slight, skimpy and somewhat superficial. Neither was he always sure where lay the boundary between attending to the day-to-day affairs of the housing society—his legitimate business—and running the personal lives of its residents—which lay outside the purview of his office. It was this brew of bluster and blunder that marred the character of an otherwise good man.

Max was not on the premises. Neither were most of the other board members, several of whom were, like Max, old-time residents of Serene Meadows, loyal to him and agreeing to whatever he brought to the table. The one member who was home told us, "If you can prove that you are free of SARS, you will receive your key." It left us wondering how we could prove we were harmless.

As I crossed the complex, trying to figure out what to do next, I ran into Gladys, the wife of George McPhee, the board member in charge of maintenance. She was tall, spare and athletic; she knew how to take charge. George, on the other hand, was short and thin, balding and timid, aware of his station in life, always walking in the wake of Gladys. I figured that, if George himself had not installed the new lock on our door, he had probably supervised the work. I walked up to Gladys to ask if she could get me the desired key. As I approached her, she backed away as if from a leper and broke into a tirade, "What are you doing here! You're supposed to be in quarantine! Do you want to infect us all with SARS! Get out of here!"

I spent the following hour phoning our family physician, the Fraser Health Authority and other health agencies, explaining our dilemma, asking if they could issue a document—any kind of statement—convincing our board we did not pose a threat to the community. They all reacted with expressions of disbelief and astonishment, wondering under which rock the board of Serene Meadows had been hiding these last two months. They told us that, since there was no longer any SARS, there was no longer any agency dealing with the infection. They all felt sorry for us, but they couldn't (or wouldn't?) do anything to help us.

Our next stop was a Walk-in Health Clinic. There we were told that all SARS related issues had been dealt with by the Fraser Health Authority. They, too, felt sorry for us. They also couldn't help. By now we were very tired. We hadn't slept for about thirty hours. I was also becoming very angry and stressed out. We finally drove to the Emergency Department of our local hospital. There we got the ear of the head epidemiologist. He called our president, who had returned from his pressing business, and assured him we were harmless. After he finished his call to Max, he told us we could go home. I never got there until one week later. Before we left the hospital, the nurse in charge asked, "Is there anything else I can do for you?"

"Yes, I don't feel well," I answered. "My chest feels tight. It hurts."

"Come along," she said. She grabbed my wrist and whisked me to a nearby stretcher. She wheeled me into a cubicle, and within minutes there was a team of doctors and nurses poking, prodding and needling me. Half an hour later, I found myself in the Intensive Care Ward, hooked up to intravenous tubes and a monitor. I had suffered a moderately severe heart attack.

Ena drove home by herself, dragged our suitcases up the stairs, phoned our youngest daughter and told her what had happened. Larissa was incensed. She got in touch with the media. The following morning, reporters from the *Abbotsford News* and the *Province* newspapers and Global Television descended upon Serene Meadows to interview Ena and the president of our board.

It was probably not the most propitious time to interview Ena. She was jet-lagged, tired and emotionally upset. When one of the reporters asked her how she felt about the Serene Meadows community, she blurted out, "Right now, I would like to get away from it as far and quickly as possible." It was an answer given to a leading question, a response made under considerable stress, a reply uttered impulsively. It was also a reaction that would add greatly to our problems in the following months.

The reporters grilled Max, questioning the appropriateness of his actions and his competency. He did not give an inch, put up a spirited defense of his handling the 'Van Dam case' and even asserted he wouldn't do anything differently if faced with a similar situation in the future. His statements drew from those who heard him remarks about condominium czars trying to run the lives of people rather than the places where they live.

Max soon realized that something needed to be done to regain face. He told his board that Ena's statement represented a slap in the face of the Serene Meadows community, and that it constituted a public resignation by the Van Dams from that community. What followed was an administration of intimidation. At a series of meetings, a plan was hatched and set in motion to force us to move. A date was set by which we should vacate our apartment. Of those proceedings, little was recorded in the minutes distributed to the residents, as required by the constitution of the society. Hardly any mention was made of the correspondence between our lawyer and the board. Our neighbors were kept in the dark about the machinations of the board. Some of the board members weakly wondered about the legality of what they were doing, but out of loyalty to the chief, they agreed to his decisions.

At last, two members resigned in protest. One of them began to speak out to the other residents. They became alarmed. They reasoned that what was happening to us could someday happen to them, and they began to explore ways in which they could legally dismiss the board. When Max and his staunchest supporters got wind of their plans, they handed in their resignation, giving "much verbal abuse by a small group of residents" as reason for throwing in the towel. It was November 11, Armistice Day—a peace of sorts settled over Serene Meadows.

A heart attack is not just a physical trauma, a reaction of the heart to the clogging of its arteries, starving its muscle of blood and oxygen, causing it to fail and leaving its victim weakened and dependent on medication for the rest of his life. It is also an affective experience in which the self reacts to an injury to the body, setting off a series of emotional responses: disbelief and denial, anger and impotence and, finally, resignation and acceptance. Recovering from the physical blow and emotional upheaval brought on by my heart attack was hindered greatly by the actions of the board, leaving me confused and discouraged, frustrated and apathetic. It was not until after our struggle with the board was well behind us, that I began to regain some of my physical strength and interest in those things that had kept me occupied before: volunteering my time, energy and expertise at the Home of Loving Faithfulness.

In early January, I visited my cardiologist. Doctor Kim—young, cocky and blunt, at times lacking in bedside manners but respected by his colleagues for his competence—told me after he had examined me, "Mr. Van Dam, you've made a remarkably good recovery. There is no longer a need for me to see you every month. Unless you develop some serious trouble, I don't want to see you until next January."

"What about travel," I asked, "is it alright for me to travel abroad?"

"Sure, why not. Where do you want to go?"

"We want to go to Hong Kong for three months."

"You like Hong Kong? I don't care for it, too busy, but they do have some good hospitals and doctors there. Get yourself adequate travel medical insurance—not that it will cover any heart problems—preexisting condition, you know. Bon voyage!" He got up, shook my hand and opened the door of his office, inviting me to leave.

"Thanks, doctor!" Feeling as if walking on air, I almost skipped to the waiting room, where Ena was paging through a dated and dog-eared copy of Readers Digest.

"What are you grinning about?" she asked. "You're smiling like a cat, who just swallowed a canary."

"Let's go, everything's fine! We're going home, phone our travel agent and order tickets for Hong Kong!"

Ms Tsang King, proprietor of Tokui Travel, is one of many who before July 1, 1997[11], moved from Hong Kong to Canada and settled in Richmond. Her office, located on the seventh floor of a commercial building on the corner of No 3 Road and Westminster Highway, is long and narrow. Those areas of its walls not covered by shelves filled with binders and travel catalogs display Bible texts in both English and Chinese. She is much interested in the work Ena and I are doing in the Home of Loving Faithfulness, and she always gives us the best possible deals.

This time, too, she didn't disappoint us. As soon as we got home I called her. She immediately recognized my voice and chirped, "Oh, hi Bill, you and Ena go to Hong Kong again? When you want to go?" I gave her some approximate dates, and she said, "I look for good deal for you. I e-mail you." Two days later we booked a flight with Cathay Pacific. From February 3 till May 4 we hoped to be in our home away from home again.

I now had to prepare for three months of teaching Sze Sze. Much valuable time had been lost. I needed to evaluate the work I had done with her and list what she could and could not do, what had and had not worked and what her strengths and weaknesses were. Guided by that assessment, I got to work on designing lessons, breaking down the process of teaching language arts into its smallest possible steps. I didn't get as much done as I had hoped, but when the time came for us to leave I had enough to get started.

Chapter 6

Although Ena and I live comfortably off our pensions and investments, we do not consider ourselves rich in earthly goods; we do not spend carelessly what took us long to accumulate. Therefore, in the past, we had not booked the more expensive direct flights from Vancouver to Hong Kong. After my heart attack, however, we agreed my health was more important than our savings, and we booked a direct flight. I discovered that even a nonstop flight proved to be long and tiring.

    I am not as fortunate as many of our Chinese friends. They can sleep anytime and anywhere, on bus, train or plane, in a comfortable bed, an easy chair or a hard wooden floor. I am one of those unlucky people, who is unable to sleep on anything that moves, no matter how long the journey, how exhausted my body, how tired my mind or how burning my eyes. But once we had landed, cleared immigration and claimed our luggage, we seemed refreshed and were excited to meet Kim in the Arrivals Hall. He was genuinely happy to see us. "I heard of your heart attack. I thought you would never come to see us again," he said in his clipped staccato. "God is good, isn't he," he added. Then, turning to Ena, he remarked, "You look good. You put on weight, he-he." To our Chinese friends, looking well-fed and being healthy are synonymous concepts, and telling friends they have packed on pounds is considered a compliment. He led us to the car park, and we loaded our suitcases into the van. On the drive home, we pumped Kim for information; we wanted to know all about the things that had happened at the home in our absence.

    We got home at half past nine. Most of the staff had gone home, to their rooms or to bed—the day starts early in the home. Only one person was still busy, Ah Lee who was on night duty. The nurse on call had already retired to her room. It was only after Kim had loaded our suitcases on a trolley and walked past the elevator, that he told us about a surprise awaiting us. Instead of the small room on the second floor, where we had lived during earlier visits, we would now have the whole Lower Ark as our living quarters.

The Home of Loving Faithfulness, a complex of connected buildings surrounding a play area, is built onto a rambling, old structure containing offices and a chapel on the first and two apartments on the second floor. It was purchased in the early seventies. Built onto it are a number of newer structures. Just off the car park are storage facilities and a work shop, above which is the well-equipped laundry room where Lita rules supreme. The ground floor of the first residential block consists of a dining room, kitchen and washrooms for staff members. The second block is made up of the Play Room, where the kids spend the day and are fed, a large and a small bedroom, a bathing and washroom area and a small dispensary. On the second floors of both these blocks are the living quarters of the Aunties and nurse, bedrooms for the in-residence staff, guestrooms, lounges, two small kitchens and communal bathing and washroom areas for staff and guests.

The Ark, the last block added to the complex, is separate from the rest of the home, not structurally but conceptually. The second block is the permanent home for the severely disabled members of the family. They live there until the Lord calls them home. The Ark is a temporary home for mostly Down Syndrome children. They live in a family setting, a transitional stage between institutional and family living, a preparation for adoption into their 'forever families'.

Upstairs, Uncle Pete and Auntie Sue, a couple from England, were the house parents for girls. Downstairs was the home for adoptable boys. Soon after our first visit to the home, its house mother adopted Matthew, a bright, eleven-year-old, suffering from brittle bone disease, and moved back to England with him. A year later, her successor adopted the last of the Down Syndrome boys and took him to her native New Zealand. That left the lower deck of the Ark vacant. The Aunties needed time to determine what to do next with this space and had decided that, for the time being, we could use it. Our bedroom was the largest in the flat and had a bathroom *en suite*. We also had the run of a large sitting-dining room and the use of a roomy, well-equipped kitchen and a laundry room. What luxury! We quickly unpacked our suitcases and went to bed.

Early the following day, after chapel service—we hadn't slept as well and long as we had hoped—we went to the Play Room. Behind the curtained doorways to the bedrooms, we could hear the cheery chatter of care givers, the sweet giggles of Siu Ping, the

Sze Sze, My Daughter

good-natured grunts of Wai Ching and the discordant banging of toys on bedrails by Wing Kit and Tak Tak. Ena disappeared behind one of the curtains and received an uproarious welcome from Shaan Shaan and Dib Dib. I would have to wait until all the members of the family, as they became ready—pottied and bathed, diapered and dressed—were wheeled into the Play Room. Attempts are made, not always successfully or consistently, rather selectively, to protect the dignity of the family. I decided to wait in our apartment. I wanted to take stock of what was there for our use. I set up my laptop and portable printer and discovered, to my delight, there was internet access in the flat.

It is commendable that the home has a policy to protect the dignity of those who are unable to do so for themselves. It is the responsibility of those who care for the disabled to respect and protect their privacy, even if they are not aware they have a dignity that needs to be shielded from disdain. The staff is very protective of the dignity of the female members of the family. Safeguarding the privacy of the male residents, however, leaves something to be desired. One evening when we were making the rounds for devotions, Ena and I were asked to wait because the person in charge was still changing Fu Fu's nappy. I could hear her explain to someone else in the room that the blood in his diaper was probably caused by kidney stones. After about five minutes, the curtain opened and out walked Tilly, she was a volunteer who worked in the Upper Ark, someone who had nothing to do with the care of the family in the Big Unit. Apparently, it was acceptable to have a teen-aged girl gawk at a forty-year-old man while he was being changed and learn all about his medical problems.

After Ena reappeared from behind the curtain, we had breakfast. Because we did not yet have any provisions in our kitchen cupboards, we ate in the staff dining room. Over toast and tea Ena told me about the kids. All but Sze Sze were fine; she felt a bit under the weather and would spend the day in bed. From the Play Room, Shaan and Dibs could see us and were clamoring for our attention. I got up to see them. Dibs, in her exuberance, nearly jumped out of her chair; Shaan loudly cried *kai kai-ah*. She wanted me to give her a ride in the garden, but it was too cold for rides. Instead, I invited our friends to watch us finish our breakfast.

By nine thirty, those who attended schools or day centers had left, and most of the others, those who were not bedridden, had been wheeled into the Play Room. The curtains were moved aside and care givers began to amble to the dining room for breakfast. It was now safe for me to enter the bedrooms. I first visited with Sau Ming and Ngan Ying, two women confined to their beds. The former spends most of her time sleeping; the latter is completely immobile and needs to have her position changed regularly to prevent the formation of pressure ulcers. Even before I came within her range of vision, I could see a smile slowly spreading over her broad face. She had recognized my voice. In the Play Room I found Siu Ping, slumped in her chair, one index finger in her mouth, drooling, her sightless eyes vacantly staring at her tray. I walked up to her and softly sang, "You are my Ping Pong, my lovely Ping Pong." Her head came up, her finger slipped out of her mouth and she began to giggle. Uncle Bill had returned! I kissed her on the forehead and sang some more to her. Then I stopped by Wing Kit and Chi Kin and talked to them. I finally made my way to Sze Sze's bedroom. Although she was happy to see me, all she could manage was a thin smile. As the day progressed, she gradually improved, and by evening she was her happy self again.

To make the most of my time in Hong Kong, I asked Auntie Wendy if Sze Sze could stay home from the center two days a week. "If Sze Sze agrees, I will not object," she replied. Sze Sze was reluctant to stay home, and it took all my powers of persuasion to convince her that one hour in the morning, five days a week, before the Rehabus came to collect her for the center, didn't give her enough time to learn to read. I added, "Don't plan to monopolize my Saturdays, when everyone is home. It won't work, young lady. Then I want to spend time with all of the family." She finally agreed to stay home on Tuesdays and Thursdays.

Teaching got off to a fitful start. My laptop refused to read the lessons I had prepared on my desktop and saved on a floppy disk. Fortunately, I had made hard copies of the lessons, but it meant I had to retype them into my laptop. Before we had left Hong Kong the previous August, some staff members and volunteers had promised to work with my student. I had wanted to make sure she would not forget what she had learned. Little had come of those promises. The home is understaffed and volunteers can't always be relied upon. As a result, Sze Sze had forgotten much of what little she had learned. The WiVik program on her computer refused to cooperate. The scanner of the onscreen keyboard scanned rows but refused to scan columns, and the Word Q program was capricious.

The Word Expansion program did work. While we waited for Uncle Pete to iron the wrinkles out of WiVik, I made up a number of abbreviations for the expansion program, an arrangement of letters eliminating many keystrokes. An entry beginning with *x* and followed by two or three other letters would expand into a longer word or phrase when followed by a space. Type, for example, *xdbe* and hit the space bar, and the abbreviation expanded to *Dear Uncle Bill and Auntie Ena*, a suitable phrase, I thought optimistically, if Sze Sze would ever want to e-mail us. I kept adding other expansions, words and phrases suggested by our young friend. I was amazed at how quickly she memorized them. It was something that grabbed her interest, was of use to her and looked like fun. The only disadvantage to the program, I thought, was that she might rely on it more than on learning how to spell correctly.

Spelling proved to be Sze Sze's greatest stumbling block. The harder I tried to teach her how to put words together, the more I became convinced the phonetic approach was wasted on her. When she made progress in discriminating between the various vowel sounds, she stumbled in distinguishing between consonants, such as initial *d* and *t* sounds. I was at a loss. She was able to read monosyllabic words, but she seemed unable to spell them back to me. Why? Was I dealing with a disability or disinclination; was I up against a mental block or a roadblock, thrown up knowingly or subconsciously? Whatever it was, it became obvious that I needed to change my approach. I needed time to reflect on the problem facing me.

I took inventory of the things Sze Sze could do. For one thing, she could read Chinese—quite an accomplishment. How had she learned to read hundreds, no, thousands of characters? In my thoughts I went back to the early nineties, to language school in *dong bei shi fan da xue*, the Northeast Normal University in Changchun. There Ena and I had learned *Putonghua*[12], China's national language. How had we learned the two thousand characters needed to read a newspaper or simple novel? We had memorized their shapes and strokes, their sounds and tones and their various meanings. Sze Sze must have done the same, I thought. Of course, she could not reproduce sounds and tones, but she had to recognize them when she read or heard them. Why could she learn to read Chinese . . . and not? Suddenly it hit me. Of course, that was it! She had learned to read Chinese using the whole language approach, and that's how she will learn to read English, I decided.

In the past I had resisted using this method, for it does not teach students decoding skills. It teaches them to memorize the shape, sound and meaning of a word, but if ever they forget what it sounds like or stands for, they will lack the skills to reconstruct it. It also limits their reading vocabulary to those words they have memorized. On the other hand, if they master the word attack skills that the phonetic approach gives them, they will be able to decode or read any word they encounter in reading. In addition, the same skills which help them to decode new words also enable them to encode those words, to put them back together, to spell them. If Sze Sze will ever learn to read, I thought, it will likely be through the whole language method. I decided to put, for the time being, the emphasis on reading rather than on spelling, hoping to give her a taste of success in one area before approaching the next. I made up my mind to set aside my dislike for the whole language approach, discuss my ideas with Sze Sze and see what would come of it.

The next day, before Sze Sze went to Wah Sum Centre, I put my plan before her. I began, "When you were a student at Elaine Field School, did you learn to read Chinese?

Yes.

"How?" I asked. "No, let me guess. You memorized the shape of a character, its sound and tone and its meaning. Right!"

She shot me a questioning look. I could almost see the wheels in her mind turning—What is Uncle Bill up to this time?—but she did show me her tongue.

"How about learning to read English in the same way."

That idea met with a lukewarm reception. "Listen, Sze Sze," I went on, "do you want to learn how to read English?"

Yes.

"I'm sure you agree we have made little progress. It's quite hard to remember and use all the rules I've been trying to pump into your head, isn't it?"

Yes.

"So, don't you think we should try a different way, a way that may be easier?"

I had to wait some time for the tiniest tip of her tongue to show. "You're hesitating . . . you feel it's an admission of failure, don't you?"

Yes.

"Perhaps we have failed, but, you know what, we failed trying, and that's alright. Failing for not trying isn't. You could also say we've tried one way and found it's not the best way," I continued, "so, why not see if there's a better way. How about it . . . shall we give it a try?"

I waited. "Look, Sze Sze, the Rehabus will be here any minute now. Why not think it over while you're at Wah Sum and let me know when you come home."

Yes.

When the bus dropped her off at the end of the day, I could tell by the look in her eyes she had come to a decision. "The answer is . . . yes?" I half asked.

She smiled.

"Thanks! Tomorrow I'll start writing stories for you. What kind do you like, Sze Sze, adventure . . . romance . . . history . . . Bible . . .?"

Yes.

"About Jesus . . . the Old Testament . . .?"

Yes.

"Do you want me to start with the creation story?"

Yes.

"Okay, tomorrow I will start writing your first story."

So began a new, time consuming but satisfying time of teaching and learning. During my years as special needs teacher, I had found that much of the published material for my students was limited in its usefulness. Therefore, I often changed stories and adapted them to the reading level of my students. I rewrote them, using carefully controlled vocabulary. At the lowest level, I chose mostly monosyllabic words that were both phonetic and interesting. I made sure to use simple sentences not exceeding twelve to fifteen words. As my students progressed, I gradually added words with two or more syllables and increased the length and complexity of the sentences. After rewriting each story, I entered all the new words in an alphabetically arranged word list, kept track of the words I had used and added the words of succeeding stories. The process took much of my time, but it was successful.

The next day, as soon as the Rehabus had left the car park, I started rewriting the first chapter of Genesis. Keeping it simple and interesting was a challenge. The final draft was a story of almost three hundred words, one word, animals, had three syllables, fifteen had two and all the others one. The sentences varied in length from two to sixteen words. It was the simplest I could make it.

I introduced the story on a Saturday morning. "Okay, Sze Sze, let me tell you what we will be doing. You will learn to read by reading. It's like learning to swim by being thrown into the deep end of a swimming pool."

She looked at me as if to say, Have you lost your senses!

"Look," I said as I waved the Genesis story before her, "here is your story. I will explain the words to you, one paragraph at a time, read it to you and then ask *you* to read it. Get it?"

Her eyes told me she didn't.

"Of course," I went on, "I'll help you whenever you get stuck. When you get to a word you don't know, you look at me, and I will help you. When you finish the paragraph you are reading, you stick out your tongue. Then we start all over again with the next paragraph, and so on, until we get to the end of the story. Now do you get it?"

Her tongue signaled yes, but her eyes told me she didn't think much of my plan.

"At first you will need a lot of help, but the more you keep reading and rereading the story, the better things will go, until you know all the words. When you tell me you have finished reading a paragraph or story without needing any help, I will trust you, I will believe you, I will never question your honesty."

She shot me a glance as if to say, Have I ever lied to you? Sze Sze was honest. She wouldn't lie to save her life; she was too proud to prevaricate.

I introduced the story. My student showed little enthusiasm. I began writing on the white board the words of the first section of the story, pronounced them and explained their meanings where necessary. I then read it a few times for her. Now it was Sze Sze's turn, and I asked her to read. Almost immediately she ran into a word she didn't know and looked at me. I pointed at each word until I came to the word that had stumped her. I helped her, and she read on. It was slow going at first. It took a while before her tongue showed she had finished the first section. We soldiered on, one paragraph at a time.

At first she stumbled over many words, but as she got farther into the story, her interest increased. So did her retention of vocabulary. We worked intensely for about one hour. Then we took a coffee break—she likes hers sweet, with a bit of milk and one of Ena's cookies—and played a game of SKIP BO. We then headed back to our kitchen-classroom in the Ark. "Do you want to work on your computer now to practice some expansions?"

No.

"Don't tell me you want to get back to reading your story? I thought you didn't like this new way of reading."

She flashed me a big grin. It was exactly what she did want. She was beginning to taste success. When lunch time came, we had worked our way through the story several times. Each time she needed less help with vocabulary.

In the afternoon, after nap time, she wanted to get back to reading, but I told her, "No, my dear, you have hogged enough of my time and attention. I now want to spend time with the rest of the family. Shaan has been clamoring for a ride, Dib Dib is getting jealous—and then there are Fa Fa and Ping Pong, Fu Fu and Emmanuel. They also want to spend time with Uncle Bill." She looked at me, questioning me with her eyes. I smiled and assured her, "Don't worry, after all the others have had their turn, I will also give you a ride."

The following day, after Ena and I had returned from church, she gave me no rest; she wanted to go back to reading. When I wheeled her to the kitchen, I teased, "I wonder how much you remember of what you have learned yesterday. I bet you have forgotten almost everything I've taught you." She merely threw back her head and laughed. She then dug in, fully focused, her mind made up to master the passage. The moment of triumph came at her third time through. She had read the whole story without needing any help. She turned to me with a look of triumph, flung up her arms and let out a loud squeal. For the first time in her life, she had read a story in English. She could read!

Her reaction caught me totally unprepared—where was my camera, my camcorder, to record this moment of triumph, to capture that expression of joy, to picture that display of pride. It was a moment that would never repeat itself. It was a lost opportunity. For a moment I just stood there, watching, unsuccessfully pushing back tears, appreciating what this meant for my disabled friend. She had humored and aging teacher, put up with his strange ideas, yet trusted him enough to go along with his odd notions. She had faced numerous, seemingly insurmountable obstacles and overcome. This was her moment!

Was Sze Sze really able to read this story? Had she, by going over it numerous times and being constantly corrected, memorized it? How did I know she was reading? How could I be sure that she was reading what I hoped she did? After all, there was no way I could verify she was reading because she was unable to verbalize. Yet, I was sure she could. I knew her. I trusted her. And that display of joy, pride and triumph I had just witnessed—could she have faked it? No, it was real!

Sze Sze reading a Bible story

Now, many years later, looking back on that moment and being sure of her fine memory, I believe that she had probably memorized much of that creation story, but that was all part of the process of whole language learning. By associating the shapes of the words on the page, the visual clues, with their sounds and meanings each time her eyes went over them, they became embedded in her memory. It was the way she acquired her reading vocabulary and learned to read.

Sze Sze was on a roll. She had tasted success. She wanted more, and there was no stopping her. We started on the second story, the narrative of the creation of Adam and Eve, and we were making good progress, but when we came to the middle of the story, where God pronounced the penalty for eating of the forbidden fruit, she stopped reading. Tears began to course down her cheeks.

Sze Sze, My Daughter

"What is it, Sze Sze," I asked, "is the thought of death making you sad?"

Yes.

"Are you thinking of someone who has died . . . your friend Yin Fan?"

Yes.

"I thought so. I'm sure you miss her a lot. It's okay to feel sad when you miss someone you loved, someone who has died. Remember how difficult her life was, especially toward the end. Isn't it good to know she loved Jesus—Where do you think she is now?"

She rolled up her eyes in that special way she has to indicate Jesus, prayer and heaven.

"Yes, Yin Fan is in heaven with Jesus, and you know what," I continued, "she is very happy there. When she gets her new body, she will be able to walk and dance, talk and sing, and do all the things she couldn't do when she was with us—all the things you hope to do when you get to heaven and meet Jesus. You will be doing all those things together with Yin Fan when you meet her there.

That thought brought a smile to her face. I reached for a Kleenex and wiped away her tears.

Chapter 7

Except for her physical disability, Sze Sze is much like any other person. She is interested in what happens in the confined and controlled world of the home where she lives and the day center she attends. She is also concerned about those who are part of that world and sensitive to their feelings. She follows the affairs of the world at large on television and struggles with the same fears and anxieties that beset others. Despite her severe physical disabilities and her keen awareness of what life could have been for her, she generally shows a positive attitude and possesses a cheerful nature. Although, as a rule, she is emotionally stable, like other teenagers, she has occasional mood swings. Like other believers, she has her spiritual highs and lows, but her faith is tried, strong and sure. She also has a healthy sense of humor and likes to tease those she loves.

In one thing she is different from many others her age: she can be very serious and pensive. Long days confined to a wheelchair, times when others are too busy to pay attention, give her plenty of pause for reflection. I have often wondered what goes on behind that high forehead of hers, what thoughts, imaginations and experiences, real or vicarious, make up her private world, a world she carefully protects.

One day, coming home from the center, she seemed very quiet. I wheeled her to the Play Room and began to feed her. She ate very slowly. I tried to find out what was troubling her and asked, "Are you tired?"

No.

"In pain?"

No.

"No appetite?"

No.

"Having a down day?"

Yes.

"Want to tell me about it?"

No.

"Well, it happens to all of us from time to time," I nonchalantly remarked. "If ever you see me when I'm down at the mouth, just ignore me. It'll blow over." That remark earned me a silent rebuke. She looked at me as if to say, Do you really think you know me? Then she rolled up her eyes. I felt chastened. This wasn't the first time she had put me in my place. "Oh . . . uh . . . you wouldn't . . . would you," I burbled. "You'd pray for me . . . I'm sorry, Sze Sze, I wasn't very sensitive, was I? Please, forgive me."

She smiled.

Something else happened around that time that shows her concern for others. Early one morning, one of the workers in the home, a woman from Mainland China, in Hong Kong on a work permit, had been caught red-handed stealing supplies from the home. She was dismissed on the spot and told to leave. She refused. The director of the home then told her that if she had not left by eight o'clock, the police would be called in and she would be charged with theft. Instead of leaving, she went to her room. One of the Aunties followed her and guarded her door. By eight she had not left, and the police was called. When they opened the door of her room, she was no longer there. She had gone onto the balcony and fled. Sze Sze had heard other staff members talk about this incident and was very upset about it.

We had put spelling on the back burner, but we continued to work with expansions. When we had about thirty of them, I decided to test Sze Sze on how well she knew them. We spent some time reviewing them, but, for some strange reason, she seemed to have forgotten most of them. She appeared less concerned about her lapse of memory than I was; she still wanted to take the test the following day. The next day, wondering how she would do and being more than a bit concerned, I administered the test. Sze Sze looked confident and not at all apprehensive. I was much surprised and very pleased with the outcome. When I told Sze Sze she had a perfect score, she looked at me with a mischievous sparkle in her eye and burst out laughing. "What did you have for breakfast this morning, brain food?" I asked. Her response was another gale of laughter. "Tell me, rascal, did you fake it yesterday?" I demanded in mock indignation. She had so much fun that she could not bring out her tongue.

After a number of weeks, my intense involvement in Sze Sze's life began to tell on me. I was not yet as strong as I had thought. I began to experience fatigue, periods of pressure on my chest and bouts of angina, symptoms cautioning me to slow down. Ena and I took the day off and did some shopping in Sheung Shui. In the Landmark North shopping center we dropped in at Delifrance where, at a table near a window overlooking the busy bus terminal and railway station, we ordered coffee and pastries and planned a short vacation. We figured that a few days of relaxation on one of the outlying islands would do me good. We decided against Cheung Chau Island because we had visited it a number of times during our China years. Instead, we opted for Lamma Island. We went home, packed a small suitcase and decided to travel the next day.

The following day we hitched a ride with Kim. After he had dropped off some of the kids at Sarah Roe School, he drove us to the Kowloontong MTR station. There we descended into the bowels of the city, boarded the subway, transferred at Yau Ma Tei to the Tseun Wan Line and exited at Central. We emerged into the sunlight and walked to Pier 4 to catch the ferry to Lamma Island. A half-hour ferry ride brought us to Yung Shue Wan village on the southern tip of the island, and a twenty-minute hike along the Lamma Island Family Trail led us to Concerto Inn where we checked in.

Lamma Island is a peaceful place without any real traffic. Little put-puts, which bring supplies to businesses and hotels, and bikes make up all the traffic on the island. For two days we relaxed, hiked across the island and enjoyed good food in a variety of restaurants. Under a large, green tarp strung between trees, we savored a bowl of Grandma Lau's tofu fa, reputed to be the best in Hong Kong. In the evening, we sat back with a good book or watched a video. The March weather was pleasant, sunny with a light breeze. On Friday morning we noticed a change in the weather and decided to head for home. We checked out at about eight-thirty and three hours later walked through the gate of the Home of Loving Faithfulness again. I don't know how much good our outing had done for me—I still felt pressure on my chest—but it had been good for both Ena and me to be away from it all for a few days. Just being together and not having to share each other with the kids had been a welcome break.

To encourage Sze Sze in her studies, I had initiated a rewards program. A perfect score on an expansion or comprehension test would earn her ten points, and ninety or eighty percent would give her nine or eight points, respectively. When she had earned

Sze Sze, My Daughter

one hundred points, she could redeem them for ten Hong Kong dollars. Toward the end of our stay, she had earned forty dollars. They burned a hole in her piggy bank. Together with Auntie Wendy and Sze Sze, we planned a way in which she could spend her fortune. We agreed on a shopping spree at New Town Plaza, a sprawling shopping complex in Sha Tin. The outing was planned for a Saturday. To make the excursion worthwhile, Auntie Wendy released two hundred dollars from Sze Sze's personal account. Kim dropped us off at the mall at eleven and promised to pick us up at three again.

The drop off area was on the Food Fair level. Our first stop was Delifrance. There we had coffee and made our plan for the day. Next, Sze Sze showed us where she wanted to have lunch, her favorite restaurant—not ours—KFC. From there we drifted up, one floor at a time, until we came to HMV on Level 4. Our young friend became excited and decided to buy a CD. After much deliberation she settled for Beethoven's Pastoral Symphony. We added to that a boxed set of Strauss waltzes.

By now it was lunch time. We went down to the Food Fair, headed for the Colonel's kitchen and found a table easily accessible for Sze Sze's wheelchair, right beside a long queue of people waiting to place their orders. A waitress spotted us. She brought us a menu, told us to make our choices and promised to be back in a few minutes. Sze Sze wanted a chicken burger and 7up. Within a few minutes the waitress brought us our food, and I paid for our fare.

While we were waiting for our food to be served, I got things ready for Sze Sze. I tucked a bib into her neck brace to catch spills and set out the small, soft plastic cup from which she drinks. Then I dug from her bag special scissors used to cut food into bite-sized chunks. Sze Sze looked at it and frowned. I asked, "You want me to cut up your food?"

No.

"You want to bite from your burger . . . like I do?"

She shot me a big grin.

I said grace. Then I held up the burger for her, and she tucked in, her face beaming. She did well. She choked only once, when she tried to eat and laugh at the same time.

We made quite a show for those queued near our table, drawing more than a few stares. That didn't faze Sze Sze. Being used to people staring at her, she would stop chewing and stare right back at them, causing them to show a sudden and intense interest in the menu displayed on the wall.

We finished our lunch. I cleaned up Sze Sze, packed the cup, bib and flannel into the bag, and we went back to our shopping. As we moved toward the elevator, I asked, "Have you made up your mind how to spend the rest of your money?" In reply she grabbed my wrist, hooked her fingers into my watchband and tugged. "O, you want to buy a watch, eh! At what level do they sell watches . . . one . . . two . . . three . . .?"

Yes. We entered the elevator and got off at Level 3. Sze Sze showed the direction and led us to a jewelry store. Of the watches on display, none were priced for less than six thousand dollars. We laughed and told her she had expensive tastes. One of the clerks directed us to a place just around the corner where they sold more affordable models. Sze Sze chose an Adidas watch for one hundred eighty dollars, ten dollars more than she had left. We gave her a ten, and she became the proud owner of a time piece. For the rest of the afternoon she kept looking at it, checking the time.

Time flies when you are enjoying yourself, and the hours allotted us for shopping quickly passed. At about a quarter to three, Sze Sze once more checked her watch and looked at me to let me know our time was almost up. We went down to the ground floor level and crossed the Food Fair to the exit. As we passed through the wide, plate glass doors, our bus arrived. Kim wheeled Sze Sze's chair onto the lift, hoisted it into the bus and secured it. We drove home in silence. Sze Sze was not the only one who was tired. This little excursion made me realize how much my heart attack had taken from me.

On Sunday morning, Sze Sze was wheeled early into our flat. She was eager to tell me something, and I asked her to use her communication board to tell me what it was. It took her fifteen frustrating minutes to let me know she wanted me to get her new watch from her room.

In the bedroom, I found Ah Lee and asked her if she had seen Sze Sze's new watch. "I think in here," she replied, pointing at Sze Sze's chest of drawers across the room. "She not buy another watch. She has many watch—you look."

I started to dig through Sze Sze's treasures. I found her new watch and discovered six more. I was laughing hard when I came back to our flat. I showed her what I had found in her drawer and asked, "Did you really need to buy another watch—which one do you want to wear today?"

Sze Sze, My Daughter

Ena asked, "What's wrong with having seven watches? Imelda Markos had three hundred pairs of shoes. Why shouldn't Sze Sze have a different watch for each day of the week?"

After we had finished laughing, I turned serious and said, "You know, Sze Sze, it took you a long time to tell me you wanted me to get your watch. I don't know whether to be angry or sad—you couldn't even spell part of the word watch. You didn't even know its first letter. At times I wonder if you *can't* or *refuse* to learn how to spell—but we'll talk more about this another time. Auntie Ena and I have to go to church now. We kissed her and left.

Although our emphasis had been on reading, we had not completely abandoned spelling. However, when it became more and more evident that she resisted learning how to spell, I had banned Sze Sze from using her computer because she considered spelling time play time. A few days after it had taken her so long to tell me that she wanted me to get her watch, I asked her, "Remember the letter to your friend Sarah you started a few weeks ago? How about finishing it—Let me turn on your computer."

She became so excited, that I had trouble strapping on her splint. I finally got her relaxed and she settled down to work. Thirty minutes later she had three words to show for all her effort. I shut down her computer, undid her splint and sat across from her to discuss our impasse. At first she refused to respond to my questions, looking away from me, but after a while she admitted that she deliberately frustrated our spelling lessons. She claimed she was afraid of failure. I responded, "Do you really believe you can't learn how to spell?"

Yes.

"You find spelling quite hard, don't you, much more difficult than reading. Well, you are right. I admit it's more difficult to put words together than it is to recognize them, but it's not impossible, you know. I'm sure you can do better." I looked at her and continued, "We've used the new way of reading for almost two and a half months now. Do you have any idea how many words you have learned to read in that short time?" She looked at me questioningly. "Almost six hundred—you have an excellent memory. With this kind of memory, you should be able to do better in spelling than you've done so far, don't you think so?"

There was no response.

"I have a feeling there's more to it than this fear of failure—it's not like you to resist, to deliberately make life miserable for yourself and me. Do you want to tell me about it?"

No. She probably did not see her way clear to express what made her act the way she did. I would have to dig it out of her.

A few days later I unearthed what Sze Sze could or would not share with me. As we came closer to the end of our visit, she became more and more difficult to deal with. She became increasingly uncommunicative. One evening she indicated she didn't want to go to bed after she had been fed her evening meal. I thought, You are right—why should a nineteen-year old be put to bed at four-thirty. We took her to our flat and played SKIP BO. After she had won all three games, and before I was going to wheel her to her bedroom, I asked the question I often put to her at the end of the day: "Did you have a good day, Sze Sze?"

No.

"A bad one?"

No.

"So-so?"

No.

"You don't want to tell me?"

No response. I reacted, "Listen, Sze Sze—look at me!—I've often told you that you have the right to keep things to yourself, especially private thoughts, but there is nothing really private about sharing with a friend what kind of day you have had, is there?"

Again, there was no response. "Why do you not want to talk to me, have I offended you?"

No.

"Is it because I ask so many questions?"

Yes.

"Too many?"

Her answer was again affirmative. "You are wrong, my dear friend. If I would never ask you any questions, would you be able to tell me what's in your heart and mind?"

No.

A thought struck me. It came to me as a shock. I had to pursue it to see if I was right. "Are you telling me that you don't want me to know what you are thinking?"

Yes.

"Do you still trust this old man?"

She gave me a troubled look but stuck out her tongue. "Thanks, I appreciate that. Now, listen carefully, Sze Sze, I'm going to say things that may be painful—not just to you, to me also. I know you trust me enough that I will not say things simply to hurt you—I love

Sze Sze, My Daughter

you too much for that—I want to help you." I waited and watched her. When I thought it was safe, I went on, "Sze Sze, you have lived so long in your own little world, in the prison of your body, you are afraid of what lies beyond its walls, aren't you? You have learned to read, and those walls have moved back a few inches. Now, if you also learn to spell, to write, to express yourself more clearly, you are afraid that the world out there will invade your space and take it over. Your thoughts, your wishes and your privacy—all the things you are protecting so carefully—will be gone."

As I was speaking, I watched her with compassion and saw that her eyes were beginning to brim and her resistance melting. "By learning how to express yourself, your world will grow bigger—it will expand, it will give you a freedom you've never before experienced." I put my hand on her shoulder and asked, "Do you fear that freedom, Sze Sze? . . . Are you afraid you will not be able to handle so much liberty?"

Sze Sze broke down uncontrollably. It was difficult to place my arms around her to give her comfort, tied as she was against the back of her chair by straps and restraints. It was equally hard to console her, fettered as she was to her circumscribed world by her anxieties and fears. I took both her hands in mine, "Listen, dear friend, I think I understand. You are not any different from anyone else. For many people, nothing is as frightening as change. Things as they are—no matter how miserable—feel familiar. It is the unknown that scares them. They fear how their lives may change—even when for the better. When well-known things give way to unfamiliar circumstances, they cling to the old and known ways."

She looked at me. For a moment her eyes told me, You understand. Then they returned to their former, troubled expression. I resumed, "Sze Sze, you will need much understanding and guidance, support and prayer as the walls of your world are pushed back. You can always count on me to help you, to give you advice and to pray with you. However, when all is said and done, it will be up to you, and you alone, to decide how much—if any—you will allow your own little world to grow. It will be your decision how much of the big world out there you will allow to invade your private domain."

She composed herself, and I refreshed her face. After we had prayed together, I brought her to her bedroom.

One day I found a forlorn Sze Sze in the Play Room. By now I was quite adept at reading in her eyes who or what was on her mind. I ventured a guess. "Are you thinking about the young man at the center?"

Yes.

I took her to the Ark, sat beside her and began, "Take a good look at me, Sze Sze. It may be hard to believe, but I was once a young man, madly in love with the most beautiful girl in the world—at least, I thought so at the time. She was the one I *had* to marry. However, although she liked me a lot, all she wanted was friendship, not marriage. I was heartbroken and wanted to put as much distance between her and myself. I left my family and country; I emigrated from the Netherlands to Canada. Most people suffer disappointments in life, and I was no exception.

She listened attentively and rolled up her eyes.

I answered, "No, I didn't ask God to help me through that difficult time. I did the opposite; I started to run with the wrong crowd and began to drink more than was good for me. I'm afraid I was not a very good Christian at that time."

She looked at me. Serious. Her tongue slid out and her eyes said, I can identify with that.

"Are you telling me you are not a good Christian?"

Yes. I did not want to interrupt the flow of my narration and intended to ask her later why she thought she wasn't a good Christian. When I had finished my story, I forgot.

The following Saturday we had pancakes for breakfast. We gathered Dibs, Fa Fa, Shaan and Sze Sze in our kitchen for the occasion. They loved to see me flip pancakes into the air and catch them with my skillet; they also loved to eat pancakes rather than the usual oatmeal porridge for breakfast. After we had washed up the dishes, I asked Sze Sze to help me return the frying pans I had borrowed from the main kitchen. I loaded them onto her tray and wheeled her to the kitchen. We then moved on to the garden. I set myself on the edge of the barbeque pit and looked at my young friend. She looked serious, and I asked her, "Is there something that weighs heavily on your mind—something you want to share with me?"

Yes. Her hand began to move slowly over her communication board: *u . . . n . . . j . . .* and she hesitated, not being sure how to continue.

"Are you spelling *unjust*?"

Yes.

"Did someone treat you unjustly?"

Yes.

"Have I inadvertently been unfair to you . . . any of the staff . . . someone at Wah Sum . . . ?"

No.

"Can you tell me who?"

She rolled up her eyes?

"Ah . . . God . . . and now you are angry with him."

Yes. Expecting an emotional scene, I suggested we move indoors. I wheeled her into chapel, took a box of Kleenex off the piano and sat beside her. I took her hand and started, "God is unfair because He allowed your heart to stop . . . because you have to spend your whole life in a wheelchair . . . because you can't do the things you want to do—things others can do and take for granted—right!"

She tried to hold back her tears but couldn't.

What words of comfort could I offer this young woman who had been dealt such a difficult portion in life. At times I felt like she did. Why were Shaan and Ping Pong, Sze Sze and Dibs, Tak Tak and others, people we had learned to love dearly, so severely disabled? What had they done to deserve this? I was at a loss for words. I said, "I understand why you feel this way, but I will not pretend I can feel what you feel." I was groping for something to say that would make sense to her, something that would, if not give comfort, put what had happened to her in perspective. I stumbled on, "It all does seem very unfair, doesn't it, but we must believe that God is fair—or He wouldn't be God, would He—but sometimes it's difficult to understand what He is doing, isn't it? I wish I had an answer to your whys, but I don't."

It wasn't that I didn't have an answer to her why. I just didn't have an *easy* answer. Intellectually I knew the truth of Romans 8:28, that to those who love God all things work together for good, but I felt powerless to make her see—no, to experience at that moment, while she was struggling with the enormity of her handicaps, with questions of why and wherefore—that all things that happen to us are an expression of God's Fatherly love for her. How could I make her understand that He has a purpose in mind: to recreate her into the image of his Son.

Sze Sze continued to cry. Do you see that sculpture of Jesus—there on that bookcase? I went on. "I wonder if He has ever thought, It's not fair that I must die to pay for the sins of Bill and Ena, Sze Sze and all the others."

She looked up but did not stop crying. Then I remembered that earlier in the week she had told me she was not a good Christian. I asked, "Is it because you are angry with God, that you think you're not a good Christian?"

Yes.

"And now you are afraid He is angry with you, aren't you?"

Yes.

"I have good news for you. He isn't. He understands how you feel, and He loves you."

She stopped crying. Her eyes questioned me. "Let me first clean your face—you look a mess—and then I'll read you a story." I went to the WC, got some wet and dry paper towels and washed the tears, mucous and saliva off her face. "There, that looks better," I remarked as I opened the Bible. "I'm sure you know the story of Job, but let me read it to you, anyway." I read the first two chapters of Job and then put down the Bible. "I guess you knew that part of the story, but do you know what's in the next thirty-plus chapters?"

No.

"Lots of speeches. Job is asking his whys. God doesn't answer. Job is accusing God that He isn't fair. God still doesn't reply. Job is frustrated with God and angry. God remains silent. Jobs friends are accusing him of hiding some terrible sins. They say God is now punishing him for his secret wrong doings. Finally, in Chapter 38, God shows up and speaks to Job." I looked at Sze Sze and asked, "What do think He said? Did He answer any of Job's questions or reply to any of his accusations? No. Instead, He had a whole lot of questions for Job, questions Job could not answer. Now, tell me, do you think God was angry with Job for questioning his fairness?"

Sze Sze's tongue came out. "Yes, God was very angry, but he was not angry with Job. He was cross with Job's friends because they had not spoken what was right. You know, Sze Sze, God had heard every word his friend Job had spoken, even his angry words. He understood. He knew that, although Job was angry, he still loved God. He knew how much Job was hurting, and God, too, was hurting. But for reasons known to God only, reasons unknown to Job, this righteous man had to go through a time of suffering."

Sze Sze looked at me, her eyes dark with sadness, but in them was a spark of new understanding. "You know, dear friend, that is how it is with you. Although you are angry with God, I know that you still love him, and He knows it too. He understands why you are angry. He hurts as much as you do when He lets things happen to you, things neither you nor I understand, but He does have a purpose with them. You must believe this. If you don't, you will be angry forever, your anger will turn to hatred, your hatred will poison your life and you will be creating your own, private hell right here on earth."

I looked at her and asked, "Do you still think you are a bad Christian, Sze Sze? Does it make you feel better to know it's okay to be angry with God sometimes?"

She smiled through her tears.

This incident moved me to take on a new task: the writing of devotions. For some time, I had been using *Devotions for Teens*, the only devotional for young people in the home, and I had been rather dissatisfied with it. It dealt with problems and temptations healthy, able-bodied, North Americans teens face in a society and culture completely alien to Sze Sze's—challenges she would never have to face in her restricted world. She needed help with questions of a different kind: living with multiple handicaps; questions about God, his love, his justice and grace; finding sources of strength, encouragement and endurance. What better source to draw on than the book of Job. I resolved to write a series of devotions based on passages from that book and apply them to her situation and circumstances. It proved to be the first of many collections of devotions I would write for her in the years which followed.

Another visit to the Home of Loving Faithfulness was rapidly coming to an end. It had been a busy, exciting and emotional three months, a time in which we had accomplished a significant breakthrough in reading but had met with considerable frustration in spelling. It had also been a period in which I had gained a deeper understanding in the complex character of Sze Sze, attained a greater awareness of the challenges and struggles, physical, emotional and spiritual, facing her and obtained a higher respect for the courage of this beautiful person whom God had given an incredibly hard row to hoe.

We left Hong Kong on a Tuesday, one of what used to be Sze Sze's stay-at-home days. However, the care giver in charge of her had not taken note of our departure and had failed to get her ready for the center. Therefore, when the Rehabus left the car park, it left without Sze Sze. When Auntie Wendy discovered the mistake, she said to her, "Oh, you are still around, are you. You won't mind seeing Auntie Ena and Uncle Bill off to the airport in my place, will you?" During the ride to the airport, she was subdued and held my hand. She showed a brave face when we kissed her goodbye.

Chapter 8

I'm struck by an interesting phenomenon: Whenever we arrive in Hong Kong from Western Canada, the only adjustment we have to make is to the difference in time, fifteen or sixteen hours, depending on the time of year. When we reverse the journey, however, we have to adjust to the relative inactivity of life in a retirement community as well as the difference in time. We miss the interaction with the family. After we have unpacked our suitcases and laundered our clothes, after we have arranged our shorts on shelves and our socks in drawers, after we have shopped for groceries and restocked our pantry shelves and after we have collected our accumulated mail and sorted through it, we percolate a pot of coffee, help ourselves to some cookies, look at each other . . . and feel redundant.

One of the first things we do is call upon our neighbors, Bud and Bess, to let them know that we have returned from the, for them, mysterious Orient. Bud is a gentle giant, a burly, good-natured fellow, a retired lumberjack who spent most of his life falling trees in the interior of British Columbia. Bess is the outspoken, no-nonsense member of the board of Serene Meadows Housing Society who, in protest to Maximilian's abuse of privilege, resigned in disgust and indignation, precipitating his fall from the pinnacle of power. With Max and his ilk removed from the board, Bess has been reelected to the board. We cross the hallway separating their apartment from ours and knock.

Bud opens the door. His broad face breaks open in a welcoming smile, and he exclaims, "Hey, Bess, look who's back; it's Bill 'n Ena!"

"Well, f'r goodness sakes, it's Bill 'n Ena. Come on in. How's China?" We enter and are hugged—Bess is the hugging type. "Sit down . . . coffee's on, let me pour y'a cup."

"Ya," Bud echoes, "sit down an' tell us all 'bout China. How's the weather out there?"

"Nice," Ena replies, "we usually wear shorts and tees."

"We've had lots o' rain here," Bud rumbles.

Sze Sze, My Daughter

"Well, what's new and exciting in Serene Meadows?" I ask. "Anything happen lately?"

"Now, let's see . . . uh . . . say, Bess, what's been hap'nin' here?"

"Let's see . . . nobody's died while you were gone, did they now, Bud."

"No, nobody's died."

"That's encouraging," Ena replies. "Anything else not happening?"

"Board meetings are pretty tame since Max is gone. Everything's goin' just fine. Say, Bud, what *has* happened since Bill 'n Ena left ten weeks ago?"

"Ten weeks, eh! My, doesn't time fly! I guess nothin's really happened."

"Take sugar 'n cream in y'r coffee."

"We're fine, Bess, we drink it black."

I guess that sums it up: Nothing really happened while we were gone nor will while we are at home.

We were not completely idle, though; Sze Sze had made sure of that. Before we left Hong Kong, she had asked us for a doll to give to her niece. Yes, Sze Sze is an auntie and very fond of her niece. We felt creative and decided to make rather than buy a doll. In the public library we found a book on making ragdolls and in a fabric store the needed materials. We got to work following the pattern but were disappointed with the results. After modifying the pattern, we came up with something quite attractive. I embroidered on it an oriental face and attached to it long strands of black yarn for braids. From patterned Chinese fabric, Ena fashioned a traditional Chinese jacket. Black trousers and cotton shoes completed the outfit. The finished doll looked like a Chinese peasant girl. A few weeks after we had mailed it to Hong Kong, we received an e-mail from Auntie Val telling us that Sze Sze had kept the doll for herself because Auntie Ena and Uncle Bill had made it. Her niece was given a substitute.

Sze Sze, My Daughter

Sze Sze, Auntie Ena and Chinese doll

Sewing a ragdoll and writing devotions on *Job* filled only part of my time. I still had too much time to think, to feel and to imagine. I felt depressed. I still felt pressure on my chest—Is it my heart, I wondered, or something else? Sometimes I felt angina and other things I hadn't noticed in Hong Kong—or had I ignored them? I am not a hypochondriac—I never used to be, I think. It's just that since my heart attack I have become more careful about my health—or is it paranoid? Because of all those symptoms, real or imagined, time at home became maintenance time. I made an appointment with our family doctor, who referred me to a medical laboratory for tests and specialists for further examinations. By the time we had been home for two months, all the reports were in. The colonoscopy showed nothing more serious than diverticulosis; the endoscopy didn't reveal any stomach ulcers, just sensitivity of the stomach to all the heart medication I am taking. Some more pills will take care of that problem—or will more pills aggravate it? Doctor Kim assured me my angina was caused by anxiety about my health problems, real or imagined. With all those reassurances, I felt fine again and was ready for another three months in Hong Kong, but since we do not like the heat and humidity of the Hong Kong summer, we decided to wait.

Time passes ever so slowly when you are waiting for something you long for to happen. However, by mid-September, staff and family members welcomed us back to the Home of Loving Faithfulness.

Sze Sze, My Daughter

We had flown EVA, a Taiwanese carrier, and arrived at a different time, midmorning rather than late evening. After we had unpacked our suitcases and made ourselves comfortable on the lower deck of the Ark, it was time to welcome Dibs and Sze Sze home from Wah Sum. In the evening I did my first devotion on *Job* with Sze Sze.

While we were home in Canada, Priscilla, Uncle Pete's office assistant, had regularly worked with Sze Sze. I had forwarded to her new Bible stories, and she had introduced them to my student. The day after our arrival, I met with Priscilla to find out how Sze Sze had done. She had refused to do any of the spelling lessons I had prepared. When I met sometime later with my headstrong friend, I found she had forgotten much of what little she had learned. At first, she had done well in reading, but as the time of our return approached, she had refused to read with Priscilla the last four stories I had sent. She had wanted to read them with me.

The next day, when I met with my strong-willed friend, I wanted to know her intentions for the coming three months. I wheeled her into the kitchen of our flat, pulled up a chair, sat down facing her and began, "I have two questions for you, Sze Sze. First of all, will you be staying home from the center again two days a week?"

There was no response.

"Are you telling me you will not stay home?"

Again there was no response from her.

"Next question, do you want to learn how to spell, write and express yourself better?"

Once more she chose to ignore my question. "Come to think of it, Miss Chan," I went on, "I have a third question for you. Do you know the meaning of the word maturity?"

She looked at me, surprised, and indicated she didn't.

"Before I began to teach you a few years ago, we had a chat together. We agreed on a way we would deal with each other. I promised I would treat you like a normal person, and we promised each other that we would respect and trust each other. Remember?"

Yes.

"Do you also remember *why* we agreed on this?" I continued. "It was because I believed there is nothing seriously wrong with your mind, and I considered you to be a responsible adult. Therefore I have always treated you as one. I hope I was not mistaken in thinking of you as a mature person. Someone is considered mature when she acts in accordance with her age. In a few months you will turn twenty; then you will no longer be a girl—a teenager—you'll be a young woman. Ignoring my questions and refusing to discuss your intentions is not acting like a mature adult. I've always treated you as an adult, I expect you to behave like one."

Sze Sze looked crestfallen. "I will now bring you back to the Play Room. Think about what I've said. Tomorrow we'll talk some more."

The next day, Sze Sze and I sat down and talked about some of the issues we had discussed the last time we were in Hong Kong: her desire to get out of the box and her fears of making herself vulnerable. I then disclosed my intentions, "I have a plan for the next three months, Sze Sze. I want to continue with your reading program. You are doing well, and I want to strengthen you reading skills. I also want to try a different way of teaching spelling. Furthermore, I want to look for a better way for you to access your computer." I looked at her closely for her reaction. There was little. I went on, "I can't do this alone; I will need your help, Sze Sze, because it will mean a lot of hard work for both of us. I promise to work hard if you promise to do the same. But before I do anything at all, I want to know what *you* want. I expect from you a firm commitment. You understand that, don't you?"

She showed me the tiniest tip of her tongue.

"If you decide to commit yourself to this, you will need to stay home from the center two days a week—Oh, by the way," I interrupted myself, "I want to remind you of another promise I made. I promised to respect your choices, even if I don't agree with them. That promise still stands."

Yes.

"So, if you feel you've learned enough, that you just want to keep up your reading skills but don't want to learn how to express yourself through writing, I will respect that choice. I will not twist your arm to make you change your mind."

Yes.

"It will not make me love you less. We will still be good friends, but it means that I will divide my time equally between all members of the family. Until now you've enjoyed special treatment. Because we needed the time to teach and learn, I've spent more time with you than with the others."

Sze Sze looked at me intently. Then she rolled up her eyes.

"You want us to pray about this?"

Yes. We did. Then I told her to think about it. "Will you let me know by tomorrow?"

Yes.

The next day Sze Sze gave me her answer. She would again stay home Tuesdays and Thursdays. She would also give spelling another serious try.

On the first day she was home we did some reading. I asked her to read a number of familiar stories and then tested her comprehension. The results were somewhat disappointing. When I analyzed them, an interesting pattern emerged. She did well on True or False and Multiple Choice questions, but what pulled down her score were questions that involved ordering or sequencing. Subsequent tests showed similar patterns.

I do not know of any tests that would give an accurate indication of Sze Sze's intelligence. Normal IQ test are very culturally based, designed for a general population living under fairly normal circumstances in a particular society, criteria that hardly apply to or describe our dear friend or her social environment. I had to gauge her acumen by what I observed in her behavior, her responses to my interaction with her and her reactions to stimuli in her surroundings. Sze Sze gives the impression of being intelligent—and she probably is—but that does not preclude any cognitive impairments, defects not normally evident in daily communication, damage done to a particular part of her brain, harm caused by the asphyxiation she suffered as baby.

Another reason why she scored low on questions involving sequencing might be a developmental disability. A child who learns to talk first utters a single word, then takes two or more and puts them in order. Soon she uses a complete, simple sentence and finally formulates assertions by sequencing a number of such sentences to express herself. It is an active, developmental process. Sze Sze's mode of communication is passive. She usually waits for someone to initiate a conversation, listens carefully to what is said, evaluates the information and then indicates assent or disagreement. Even when she wants to share a thought, she relies on the other party to guess what it is she has in mind, to formulate a statement or frame a question. Then she indicates whether or not she agrees.

Sze Sze has never had to order her words or sequence her thoughts to formulate an argument. It is typical of people in her condition to become passive communicators, initiating little communication, exhibiting a learned helplessness, something early intervention may prevent or alleviate to some degree. She was robbed of that opportunity because, as a child, she was incorrectly diagnosed as severely mentally disabled. The reason why Sze Sze scored low on questions that involved sequencing may be a combination of some or all of these factors. The more I work with her, the more she fascinates me, not as an interesting case study but as a person. The longer I deal with her, the less I seem to know her.

After a number of days working with her, I began to notice a change in Sze Sze's behavior and attitude toward me, and she refused to tell me why. One way she showed this was by refusing to be fed by me. This was highly unusual for her. In the past, whenever I fed any of the other family members, she would look at me as if to say, Aren't you supposed to feed me! She chose Ena to feed her and looked at me with defiance. It made little difference to me whether I fed her or someone else, so I chose to feed Dibs instead. She swallows food as fast as I can shovel it into her mouth. Feeding Sze Sze, however, takes time. Little spoonful of food must be placed in the left side of her mouth to prevent choking. When she does choke, whoever is feeding her may be wearing her dinner.

It did not bother me that she did not want me to feed her. What did bother me was her negative behavior and refusal to talk. When I asked her if I had offended her in any way, if there was anything in my behavior that bothered her or if there was anything at all I had done to provoke her, she told me there was nothing. After enduring a week of her rudeness, I asked her at devotion time, "Tell me, Sze Sze, are you happy about the state of our relationship?"

No.

"Shall we forget about whatever it is that drives us apart and get on with life?"

Yes. But nothing really changed.

Trying to find a reason for Sze Sze's unusual behavior, I discussed the problem with Ena. She suggested, "Perhaps Sze Sze is jealous."

"Jealous . . . jealous of who?"

"Dibs . . . Dib Dib is so easy to love. It takes so little to make her happy. She is uncomplicated. Most of the time, she is a happy camper. Once in a while she is a bit moody, but never for long—she certainly isn't manipulative, like Sze Sze is now. It's that, or she is jealous of me, of our relationship. She may be trying to play us off against each other.

"She will never admit to being envious of either Dibs or you," I replied, "but we should let her know that she can't play games, that she won't succeed in driving a wedge between us. Let's talk to her together."

Sze Sze, My Daughter

Early the following morning—it was a stay-at-home day—Sze Sze was wheeled into our flat. We were waiting for her. She probably expected to hear from me what we would be doing that day. Instead I began, "Well, Miss Chan, do you agree that things are different between us?"

Her eyes told me it was a question she had not expected. They moved from Ena to me, wondering what would come next. She slowly showed her tongue.

Whenever there is a serious issue between us, I never address Sze Sze by name. I want her to feel there is something separating us, something that should not be there. I want her to feel the emotional distance that has come between us, but I still want her to know I care for her.

I continued, "You know, my friend, as time passes, things change, situations change and people change. But whatever changes, our love for you will never change. Ena and I will always love you. You know that, don't you?"

Yes.

"Ena and I realize that you are not any different from other people. With the passing of time, you also change, and we will accept a changed you. There is, however, one change in you we will not accept, and that is a rude and uncooperative attitude."

She looked down at her tray.

"Is there anything Uncle Bill has done to offend you, has he said anything to hurt you," Ena asked, "anything at all that has caused your attitude toward him to change?"

No.

"Do you want to tell us why you behave as you do?"

No.

"Well, then we will have to guess the reason for your changed behavior," Ena continued. "I think you are jealous—jealous of Dibs . . . or of me . . . . Am I right?"

Her eyes flashed an angry no.

"Well, whatever it is, young lady, it is something I *cannot* and *will* not deal with," I interjected. "I find it difficult to teach someone who is rude and uncooperative. Therefore we will stop our lessons until I feel you are ready to be taught again."

Tears began to fill Sze Sze's eyes.

"I will not ignore you. You will still have your turn when I give the kids rides in the garden, we will still have coffee together and play games at times, but there will be no more lessons until I see a real change in your behavior."

It did not take long for Sze Sze's behavior to change. At lunch time, when Ena was feeding her, Sze Sze was eyeing me, begging me to feed her. I promised to feed her at tea time. At devotion time we talked things out. She realized she had gone too far and could not play games with Ena and me. When it was time for prayer, she didn't want me to pray with her. I asked, "Do you want Ena to pray with you?"

No.

"Do you want to pray by yourself?"

Yes.

"That's good, there's no reason why you shouldn't. No one but you knows better what your needs are."

Her eyes told me she agreed.

"Before Ena and I go back to our room, I want to know if you've had a good day."

She flashed me a big smile, happy that barriers had been cleared between us. I asked, "May I kiss you a good night, Sze Sze?" She said yes, and I wished her sweet dreams.

We have decided on a different format for our spelling lessons. Sze Sze chooses ten words from the vocabulary list of her Bible stories. I print those words and tape them to the tray of her wheelchair. All week long she has an opportunity to study them, whenever she has nothing else to do, which is much of the time she spends at Wah Sum. At the end of the week I test her. The words she misspells become part of the new spelling list. Ten words a week doesn't seem like a lot, but is more than she has done before.

Yet, I have questions about this new measure of success. Is she using the word attack skills I've been trying to sneak into the lessons by the back door, or is she simply memorizing the shape of words. I'm afraid it is the latter. She may have a perfect score on her spelling test one week, but a few weeks later many of those words have slipped out again. That she is not using word attack skills becomes especially evident when she tries to tell me something using her communication chart.

There are days when I wonder what is stirring in Sze Sze's heart and mind. One morning she seemed unusually subdued and serious. She was staring at the page before her rather than reading it. Soon tears began to roll down her cheeks. When I asked her if she wanted to tell me what it was that made her sad, she answered yes. I put aside her reader to clear her communication board, and her hand began to move over the letters, but soon she gave up. Was she unable or unwilling to spell the words she wanted to use? I don't know. She then indicated she didn't want to share with me what burdened her.

Our friendship is a curious one. First there is the difference in age. I am her senior by fifty years. Next, how well do I really know her? Sometimes I think I know my young friend. Interpreting her body language often helps me ask the right questions; it makes me feel I can read her like an open book. On other days, however, it feels like I am in the wrong library, and I have a sense I don't know her at all.

What do I really know about her beyond her physical condition and its cause? I believe there is an intelligent mind trapped in a dysfunctional body, but how sure can I be about the breadth and depth of her intelligence? I like to think she has learned to read English, but do I know this is really true? Have I ever heard her read? I know by the appropriate way she reacts to the spoken word that her listening comprehension is high, but does this translate into a similarly high level of understanding in reading? Was the failure to communicate her sorrow the other day the result of not being able to spell, or was she holding back, consciously or otherwise, for fear of making herself vulnerable? What do I *really* know of her, of her longings and fears? I am "seeing through a glass darkly."

I expressed these thoughts to her one evening at devotion time. She listened to me carefully, looked at me knowingly and agreed with me fully that I do not really know her at all. And sometimes I wonder if she wants me to know her any better than I do now. However, I cannot walk away from this unusual relationship. Sze Sze does more than just fascinate me as an interesting case study or test my abilities as special needs teacher. The feeling I harbor for her is a genuine affection—not pity disguised as love for a young woman who got a raw deal in life. I love her for who she is: a loyal and loving friend, an attractive young woman with a sparkling, magnetic personality and a sense of humor.

Yes, Sze Sze does have a sense of humor. One morning our spelling lesson was interrupted by Mia, a young Filipino nurse who has been working for a number of years as volunteer in the home. There is a close bond of friendship between Sze Sze and Mia. After some joking around, Mia asked, "Am I interrupting your lesson?"

"Yes," I answered, "we were doing a spelling lesson. You are an interruption, and interruption will be the next word I will teach Sze Sze."

"I'm sorry," Mia laughed, and she left.

Although interruption was not on Sze Sze's list of spelling words, she indicated that she wanted to learn it. We tried, but she found it too difficult, so we gave it up. Half an hour later Mia came into our classroom again and asked, "And, Sze Sze, do you know how to spell interruption already?" Before I could answer it was too difficult for her, Sze Sze stuck out her tongue and her hand began to move over the communication board. She spelled *m . . . i . . . a* and burst out laughing. Mia feigned great indignation and stormed out of the kitchen.

Spelling remained Sze Sze's great stumbling block. It was to her credit, however, that whenever I asked if she wanted to discontinue, she refused to give up. *Quit* was not part of her vocabulary. For a number of days she had been trying to tell me something, but I was unable to figure out what it was. Neither she nor I was prepared to leave it; we kept coming back to it. I finally discovered it had something to do with her birthday party the following month. "Do you want me to invite someone to your party?"

Her face broke open in a smile. Finally, Uncle Bill had caught on.

"Is it a man . . . boy . . . girl . . . woman?"

Yes.

"A lady—at Wah Sum?"

No.

"Spell her name." She couldn't.

"Have I met her?"

Yes.

"Is she a friend of yours?"

Her smile answered that question. "Well, Sze Sze, if she's a good friend, I'm sure you have a picture of her in your photo album."

Her face brightened. Finally, we were getting somewhere. I wheeled her to the bedroom, and she indicated in which drawer I could find her picture album. Digging through an accumulation of treasures, I located it near the bottom. I sat down on the edge of her bed, pulled her chair close, placed the album on her tray and began to page through it. We came near the end of the album, but there was still no indication from Sze Sze that we had come to the right picture. I asked, "Are you sure you have a picture of her?" She was. Finally, there it was, a picture of Sze Sze and a young woman. Yes, I recognized her. I had met her once or twice. Her name was Jacqueline Au Yeung, a physiotherapist at the Elaine Field School.

She was the person who had shared the good news of salvation with Sze Sze and led her to Christ.

Sze Sze and Jacqueline Au Yeung

Toward the end of our visit, frustration was beginning to show on Sze Sze. Unless we have found ourselves in a similar situation, we cannot imagine how frustrating life must be for anyone who finds it almost impossible to make her thoughts known. The closest I have come to such a predicament was in my early China days. I had ventured out to go shopping without taking with me one of my students to interpret. I was unable to find what I needed and incapable of asking for it. I well remember the feeling of impotence and frustration. To have the endurance to live under such circumstances all the time requires a special measure of courage and grace. I sometimes wondered if I was guilty of adding to Sze Sze's level of frustration. Were my expectations for her too high? Should I have been satisfied with what she had achieved in reading and back off—forget completely about teaching her how to spell?

Had she expected to pick up spelling as quickly and easily as she had reading? She is torn. On the one hand she is afraid of making herself vulnerable; on the other, she wants to be able to express her needs and wants.

There were ways in which Sze Sze worked off her frustrations—walking. Because she had outgrown Tak Tak's walker, the home had provided Sze Sze with her own walking machine. The walker is a high metal frame on little wheels. At the top there is a horseshoe shaped bar from which is suspended a canvas sling. When Sze Sze sits in it, her feet will just reach the floor. However, when she walked, her pelvis swung too much from side to side. It made walking difficult and caused her hips to hurt. Auntie Wendy designed a new sling which limited this swaying motion. It made walking easier and safer for Sze Sze.

Sze Sze had also outgrown her leg splints. They are like boots made from hard, resinous material, open at the toes and reaching to just below the knees. They come apart in two sections, one part covering her sole, heel and calf, the other protecting her instep and shin. Those parts are joined together with buckles and Velcro straps. We needed to go to the Prosthetics and Orthotics Department of Nethersole Hospital to have new ones made. Ena and I were asked to accompany Sze Sze and Mia. We were needed to push the wheelchair as well as the walking frame. To transfer Sze Sze from her chair to the frame, three people are needed.

Doctor Wong first wanted to see Sze Sze walk in her old splints. After Mia, one of the nurses and I had transferred Sze Sze to the walker, she was asked to walk while the doctor observed her gait. He was impressed by the design of the new sling. Sze Sze was then put on an examination table and the doctor took measurements for the design of the new splints. One of them needed a thicker sole to compensate for the difference in the length of her legs, caused by an operation to release the tightness in the muscles of one of her legs. A few weeks later, Ena and I once again escorted Sze Sze to Nethersole for a final fitting. With the new leg splints, walking for Sze Sze has improved considerably.

It are often the littlest things in my interaction with Sze Sze that bring the greatest joy, both to her and me. How often I have wished she could speak. How often I have longed to hear her say something I could understand, but a lack of muscle control keeps her from producing intelligible speech. Then, one day, quite unexpectedly, it happened. The food trolley was pushed into the Play

Sze Sze, My Daughter

Room, and Ena asked her, "Who is going to feed you today, Sze Sze?" Before Ena could ask, "Bill . . . me?" Sze Sze closed her lips, blew air through them and blurted "bll". We were startled. I turned to her and asked, "Did you say Bill!" She threw back her head and laughed, overjoyed she had called my name and I had understood. It was a moment of triumph for her to say my name. It was an occasion of great joy for me to hear her do it.

It is amazing how much uncontrolled power can be generated by the muscles of those who suffer from cerebral palsy. At times, when Sze Sze becomes excited or is startled, she goes into an extension, her body stiffens and tries to straighten itself. This is an extremely painful experience when she is strapped in her wheelchair, because her body, thighs and lower legs are secured to the back, seat and footrests of her chair by broad straps. The tubular frame of the chair is strong enough to withstand the enormous power created by her muscles, but something, usually the back of the chair, has to give. Twice during this three-month visit Sze Sze went into an extension. In both cases there was a loud, cracking noise, and the back of the wheelchair, made of half inch plywood, broke in two. Each time, it took me three hours to take the chair apart, make a new back, attach all the straps and hardware and put it all together again.

When we arrived in Hong Kong almost three months earlier, I had set out to accomplish three things: strengthen Sze Sze's reading skills, develop a different strategy for teaching spelling and find a better way for her to access her computer. I had been successful in reaching my first objective. She continued to make good progress in reading, increasing her reading vocabulary and enjoying the reading of stories. I had been less successful in reaching my second goal. We continued to struggle in spelling, taking two small steps forward and one giant stride back. But it was not until we had almost come to the end of our visit, that I was able to look into a better way for Sze Sze to access her computer. I received a call from one of the therapists at Wah Sum Centre, telling me about disabled students at the Princess Alexandra Red Cross Residential School. They were using a variety of devices to access computers. She was able to make an appointment to have Sze Sze assessed there. I hoped we would be successful in finding a gadget that was better than the splint she was using now to access her computer.

At the Red Cross school we were shown a variety of devices. The gadget that looked the most promising and suitable for Sze Sze was a tip switch, a deceptively simple thing, consisting of a square tube about two inches long, filled partially with mercury. In a horizontal position it completes an electrical circuit; when held vertically the contact is broken. The switch was taped to Sze Sze's forearm and plugged into a USB port of her computer. She was then asked to operate the WiVik program. Although she was under considerable pressure to perform and watched by half a dozen people, she did quite well. The school was willing to lend one of those switches to Wah Sum Centre to see how she could use it to operate the Cross Scanner, a program she used at the center to open computer programs.

One reason why the tip switch seemed attractive was that it looked like a great improvement over the arm splint. That hard plastic accessory with its micro switch, strapped to Sze Sze's forearm, proved to be a formidable weapon, requiring someone to sit constantly by her side, restricting the range of her involuntary movements, keeping her from knocking keys off the keyboard of her computer. With a tip switch taped to her arm, there would be little danger of that happening. Still, there was the problem of space on the tray of her wheelchair. I already had moved her support posts a few inches to make sure her laptop would fit between them. This left little room for Sze Sze to rest the arm on which the switch was to be taped. One solution would be putting the computer on a table near her chair, plug in a separate flat screen monitor and place that on her tray. However, before asking the home to incur this additional expense, we needed to be sure that the tip switch would solve the access problem we were wrestling with. It was unfortunate that all this came about, again, shortly before our return to Canada. I was prepared to buy a tip switch, a rather inexpensive device, once I had heard from the people at Wah Sum that Sze Sze could handle it successfully, but that would have to wait until we had returned to Hong Kong again for our next visit.

A few weeks before our return to Canada, I finished doing the devotions on *Job*. Sze Sze felt those devotions had been helpful to her and wanted me to write more. Whenever she felt sad or depressed, she wanted me to read Psalm 23, a passage of Scripture that gave her, like so many other believers, much comfort. When I asked her if she wanted me to write devotions on that psalm, her face lit up. In chapel I found Philip Keller's *A Shepherd Looks at Psalm 23*. Using that classic as guide, I started to write two-page devotions. By the time we left for Canada, I had written the first four of twelve devotions.

Sze Sze, My Daughter

Too soon the day of departure arrived. While Ena and I were finalizing our packing early that morning, Sze Sze was in her walker, cruising around our flat under supervision on one of the volunteers. Our normally quiet friend was very boisterous. Every time she came past our bedroom, she stopped to see how we were doing. She appeared happy, but I knew it was all a charade. At breakfast time, her eyes begged me to feed her, but soon she choked on her porridge and began to cry. She wanted me to take her to chapel. There she dissolved in a flood of tears. She was inconsolable. Telling her we would be back in March did little to calm her. It almost seemed as if she was afraid of never seeing me again, or as if there was something else she feared. After a time of prayer she calmed down enough for me to clean her face. I then took her to the car park and watched the Rehabus take her to the center.

Chapter 9

We came home to the usual, mid-November West Coast weather: dun and drab, wet and windy and most miserable. After being cooped up for about a week, cabin fever got the better of us. We needed to get out. We bundled up, grabbed our umbrellas and headed for Mill Lake Park. It was deserted. Cheerless cedars and melancholy cypresses shook in the wind. Broadleaf maples thrust bare branches into a lead sky, and careless cottonwoods dropped dead wood around the bases of their rain-streaked trunks. A tenacious oak clung to the last of its bronzed leaves; they were all that remained of the summer that had been. Tangled brambles huddled together for comfort. The lake was black and choppy. The dismal weather reflected our mood. It made us wonder why we had ventured out at all. We hunched in our padded jackets, leaned into the wind and hurried back home.

We felt trapped in our cramped apartment. There are only so many things one can do in a nine-hundred-square-foot home. Vacuuming carpets, mopping hard surfaces and dusting furniture took only a few hours of our time each week. Breakfast and lunch dished were rinsed, put aside and washed with the supper pots, pans and plates. Then something happened that drew attention away from the wretched weather and our disheartened selves, something that kept me from sliding into my usual homecoming depression—a series of early morning phone calls. The first one came from Auntie Wendy. Miscalculating the sixteen-hour time difference between Hong Kong and Abbotsford—counting forward rather than back— she called us out of bed at three in the morning, asking us to pray for Kim. He had been felled by a stroke that morning. Kim is more than the only person in the home who has a license to operate the bus. He also maintains the gardens around the home, does all the grocery shopping and takes care of most of the banking. He drives to the airport to welcome guests who visit the home and brings them back again after their visits, often after working hours. Having Kim felled by a stroke was a major blow to the home.

The second call came from Auntie Val. Repeating Auntie Wendy's error, she awoke us a few days later at about the same time. She asked us to remember Sze Sze in our prayers. For a number of days she had been unable to keep down any food or drink and had been admitted to the Prince of Wales Hospital for tests and observation. A third call came on the first of December, a little after midnight, telling us she had undergone emergency surgery to remove a section of necrotic tissue from her intestines. She was now recovering in the Intensive Care Unit.

Four days later, there was another midnight call. Infection had set in. Another operation had been performed to drain the infected area and construct an ileostomy, an artificial opening from the ileum through the abdominal wall, permitting the voiding of the small intestine. This process was to be reversed once the infection had been taken care of and Sze Sze would be strong enough to undergo a third surgery. Also a gastrostomy was put in place, allowing her to be fed directly into the stomach once she got off intravenous feeding. Some in the home did not think reversing the ileostomy would be desirable because of the danger of another infection or the formation of adhesions, the abnormal growing together of adjacent tissues.

I knew little of stomas of any kind. I Googled 'ileostomy' and came upon an illustrated article. It showed that in an ileostomy, the stoma is usually situated above the groin on the right side of the abdomen. If the ileostomy would not be reversed, I wondered what would happen if Sze Sze went into an extension while she was strapped in her wheelchair. The ostomy pouch would get squashed, reversing the flow of waste into the ileum, or it would burst. It would also not be possible to strap her tightly in the sling of her walker without reversing the flow. However, all this would be of later concern if Sze Sze would pull through, and it would be hers to make the decision.

We were in constant contact with the home, often calling twice a day. The news was not encouraging. Sze Sze ran a high fever and was drifting in and out of consciousness. A tube had been inserted in her throat to help her breathe. Her lips were blue and her legs swollen.

For days Sze Sze was hovering on the brink of death. I was worried. This young woman had become as precious to me as one of our own children and was continually on my mind. From the moment I woke until the time I went to sleep, I wondered how she was doing. Situations always seem more serious when we are far removed from them, and we often fear the worst. I did not sleep well and often got up in the middle of the night. Struggling with my fears and wrestling with God, I tried to make sense of what was happening to my young friend. Why was she, who had already suffered so much in her short life, singled out for this additional affliction?

One night, after one of the midnight calls, I did not return to bed. I spent much of the night in thought and prayer. Reflecting on the past three years, I pondered on my involvement in Sze Sze's life, on our unusual relationship and on our struggles and triumphs. I remembered the talks we'd had about the purpose God had for her life, and I called to mind my belief that her learning to read and express herself through writing might be preparation for carrying out that purpose. Then, suddenly, I realized that God's purpose and what I had imagined to be God's purpose might be very different. Perhaps, I feared, He had decided to call her home at this time and say, Sze Sze, you've done all I wanted you to do here on earth. You've touched the lives of many. Because of you, Bill has become a more teachable, compassionate and sensitive person. Now, come home with Me, enjoy my presence, rejoice with your friend Yin Fan and do all the things you've always longed for but were unable to do. If that happened, would I be ready to release her and rejoice with her, or would I collapse in a heap of self-pity?

I tried to pray but found it impossible—what should I pray for? I stopped in the middle of a prayer pleading for full recovery and wondered if I was fair to her—she longed so much to be with Jesus. Did I have her best interest in mind when I prayed for complete healing—she desired so much to be set free from her unresponsive body. What would life for her be like if she recovered? More of the same: Sitting in a wheelchair, having others do everything for her, waiting for others to move her from place to place, hoping it would be where she wanted to be. Is that what Sze Sze wanted? Is that what *I* wanted for her? As I was wrestling with those questions, I longed to be with her, sit at her bedside and ask her what she wanted me to pray for.

I reflected on my three years of teaching Sze Sze to read and write, on my efforts to liberate her mind from the bonds of her body and on my struggle to break open the door of her prison. What foolishness! The best I could hope for was to pry open that door just a tiny crack. That night I learned that only One could set her free, and that He will do so in his own good time.

Sze Sze, My Daughter

I thought about our friendship. Sze Sze and I had at times talked about it. We saw love between friends as one of the great gifts from God, and we cherished the bond of affection that had grown between us. That night was hard—but it was good. I went through a gamut of emotions: anger and resentment, confusion and disquiet, resignation and, finally, a deep peace. In those dark hours I learned to hold the gift of friendship loosely, became willing to return it to the Giver and be content to thank him for the time He had graciously allowed us to enjoy that gift.

In the weeks leading up to Christmas, there was little change in Sze Sze's condition. Healing of the incisions was slow. She was in great discomfort. When she was conscious, communication with her was difficult. Because she was not allowed to have anything by mouth, not even water, her mouth was very dry. Although the breathing tube had been removed, she found it difficult to bring out her tongue.

On the night of December 13, there was another three-o'clock call. I stumbled out of bed, but before I had a chance to lift the receiver from its cradle, the phone had stopped ringing. I waited a few minutes to allow the caller to record a message. I then retrieved it. It was a call from Pat Chow, the new, part time nurse at the home. She was at Sze Sze's bedside, found her in low spirits and was afraid she had lost the will to live. Although we had never met, she had heard of our deep friendship, and she wanted me to talk to Sze Sze. It was a desperate attempt to rally her flagging spirit. Pat had not left her mobile number, so I phoned the home to get it. I then called her at the hospital. While Pat held the phone to Sze Sze's ear, I talked to her for about ten minutes, encouraging her with the words of Psalm 23 and the promise that Ena and I would return to Hong Kong as soon as possible. When Sze Sze became tired, Pat got back on the phone, telling me Sze Sze was alert and smiling when she heard my voice.

In the morning, I called Tokui Travel to see what flights were available. The time leading up to Christmas and the first ten days after New Year's Day are usually busy and expensive for travel, but toward the end of the second week of the new year, sales begin to slump. EVA was having a seat sale for January 11, 18 and 25. A quick look at the calendar told me the first two dates were out because I had an appointment with the heart specialist for my annual checkup on the eighteenth. That left us the twenty-fifth. We phoned the home to ask if our coming almost two months earlier than we had planned would cause any inconvenience. Wendy replied, "Why would it—you belong here." We booked our flight, e-mailed Sze Sze and hoped this news would rouse her will to keep fighting.

The holiday season was without its usual merriment. The weather was miserable. Christmas was wet rather than white. A head cold, tenacious as a terrier, forced me to bow out of Christmas dinners and church services. Then there was Sze Sze; her condition kept our minds off the traditional Christmas cheer. Twice I checked into Emergency because of severe chest pain, but overnight tests and observations revealed there was nothing to be concerned about. A prescription of nitroglycerine patches took care of most of my angina attacks, probably caused by my anxiety and concern for Sze Sze.

And so, the year 2004 ground to a halt. On Boxing Day the world was shocked by the devastation and loss of life caused by an earthquake off the coast of Sumatra and the resulting *tsunami*. Insurance companies felicitously acknowledged it an act of God. So did some overzealous preachers, calling it God's righteous judgment on godless nations, countries where Buddha, Allah or a pantheon of Hindu deities are worshiped. Calamities like these often hit the poorer regions of the world; they strike people who can least afford the economic devastation caused by such a catastrophe. However, I wondered if the more affluent Western world, erstwhile Christian countries where the gospel has been emasculated, made redundant or declared irrelevant, was any less deserving of Divine retribution. Why were nations spared that allow the innocent to be slaughtered before they see the light of day and that make mockery of what God intends to be a family. Why have mercy upon societies that preach tolerance for all but the Christian religion.

A few days before our departure for Hong Kong I had a scare. I woke from an afternoon nap in my recliner. Ena was standing at the living room window. When she saw me awake, she exclaimed excitedly, "Look, spring must be just around the corner. I can see the first crocuses poke their spears through the soil in the neighbor's garden." I jumped up to walk to the window and stumbled. Trying to steady myself, I took another step. I noticed my left foot dropped and scraped the carpet. I felt dizzy and sat down on one of the dining room chairs. I thought, perhaps my foot is asleep, but it didn't tingle. I was perplexed and wondered if I had suffered a light stroke. After a few minutes, my head cleared, I tried to walk and everything seemed normal again, but I continued to worry and had a restless night.

The following day at the doctor's office—we needed prescriptions for our three months' supply of medications—I related to Doctor Dave what had happened the day before. I asked if he thought I had suffered a light stroke. While he checked my reflexes, he asked for details of the incident. He then reassured me all was fine. I had come close to fainting because I had moved too quickly from a reclining to an upright position, something for which I had been warned after my heart attack. When I drove to the pharmacy to have our prescriptions filled, I was reminded of a short poem by an unknown Dutch poet.

> Too oft' man suffers more
> From suffering caused by fear
> But never makes its presence,
> And thus he's forced to bear
> More than God e'er intended.[13]

Chapter 10

We landed at Hong Kong's International Airport at about ten in the morning and were welcomed by Kim and Mr. Chow. Kim had recovered well from his stroke, but he was not yet allowed to drive. He introduced us to Kit Chow, the new bus driver. On the way to Kwu Tung, Kim told us Sze Sze was back in the operating theater to have her ileostomy reversed. When we arrived at the home, we were told the surgery had gone well and she was back on the surgical ward. Later that day, Pui Yee drove us to the hospital.

It was obvious that Sze Sze was uncomfortable; her thin face was pinched with pain. Her hands were covered with shapeless mitts and tied to the bedrails to keep them from pulling at the many tubes going into and coming out of her body. While Pui Yee was busy moistening Sze Sze's mouth, greasing her lips, cooling her face and doing other things to make her comfortable, Sze Sze kept her eyes fastened on mine. Her mind was clear; she responded appropriately to my questions. At the end of our short visit, I prayed with her. She smiled through her tears, grateful we had come.

For the next three and a half weeks, we visited her almost every day. We used mostly public transport to make our way to the hospital. At the gate of the home, we'd flag down the four-thirty 51K minibus; it would take us to the Sheung Shui KCR Station. From there we'd ride the train south to Fo Tan. Finally, we'd hop on the 811 minibus and get off in front of the Prince of Wales Hospital at five-thirty. After a two-hour visit with our young friend, we reversed our journey. Halfway into our visit, we usually took a twenty-minute break at the canteen to buy a bowl of noodles or a cup of coffee to wash down the sandwiches we had made. By the time we arrived home, it was too late to say goodnight to the kids and do devotions with them.

Days for Sze Sze on the surgical ward were long. Patient care at the hospital was generally good, but there were times when nurses were too busy with taking in new patients to see how she was doing. Being unable to speak or call out, having no useful control over her

Sze Sze, My Daughter

fingers to use the call bell and finding her hands tied to the bedrails, she was unable to call, ring or motion for help when she needed it. On one such day, we found her in great distress and close to tears. She had been placed in a reclining chair that was not molded for her body. She had slid into an uncomfortable position against the side of the chair and was in pain. We called for assistance, and soon she was transferred to her bed. Our visits were the highlights of her days.

Sze Sze's recovery was slow and uneven. Some days she seemed to be making visible progress, but they were followed by times when pain and fever took over again. There were days she was discouraged by the slow pace of improvement; on other days she was in wonderful spirits and full of mischief. On one such day, when I came to the ward, she was just waking from a nap. I touched her forehead to feel if the fever of the previous day had gone down. It felt cool. I asked, "Well, Sze Sze, are you feeling any better than yesterday?"

She looked at me, frowned and answered no.

"The same?" Again I received a negative answer.

"Worse?"

Yes.

At that point in our conversation, Ena entered the ward and asked, "Feeling any better today, Sze Sze?"

She looked at me with a twinkle in her eyes, stuck out her tongue and burst out laughing. It was good to see the return of her sense of humor.

"Ah, Uncle Beel, welcome to our church! Welcome back to Hong Kong! Where's Auntie Ena, I hope she's okay!" Junko, the wife of Pastor Yoshida, shook my hand warmly as she welcomed me that first Sunday we were back in Hong Kong. Junko volunteers at the home. She is cheerful and exuberant, an accomplished pianist and an excellent soloist. On Thursday mornings, when she comes to the home to play and sing for the family, we bring all those who do not attend schools or centers into chapel and join her there.

"I'm afraid Ena is not as well as she would like to be. She is nursing a nasty cold."

When we are in Hong Kong, we worship at Cornerstone Baptist Church. A ten-minute bus ride brings us to the older part of town. After we exit minibus 17, we cut through the Buddhist open air shrine and skirt mahjong players who are already intent on their game. We then thread our way through an early morning crowd, picking over vegetables at market stalls, and exit at Tsun Fu Jie, a busy shopping street. We greet shopkeepers opening the steel shutters of their shops, cut through a short alley, turn left at Jockey Club Road and ascend a set of narrow stairs just past the car wash and garage. On the second floor landing, we pass an offering of fruit and smoldering joss sticks and move on to the third floor where services are held in a large apartment. The church draws its membership mainly from the community of Filipino and Indonesian domestic workers in the Sheung Shui area.

Ena didn't want to pass on her cold to Sze Sze, so that Sunday and the next few days I made hospital visits alone. By now I had established a routine of refreshing Sze Sze. I would wash her face with a moist cloth, clean her lips and put on Vaseline to keep them from cracking, and clean out her nostrils with cotton swabs. Then I'd rub her arms and legs with a damp flannel, all the while chatting, passing on the latest gossip from the home.

I had also learned how to visit with a patient who is unable to speak. After having her cleaned up, straightened out her bed and put her in a comfortable position—she had lost so much weight that I could easily scoop her up in my arms—I'd place a chair where she could see me, sit down and ask if she wanted me to talk or keep quiet. Sometimes she wanted me to read with her, do devotions, pray or simply chat. That Sunday, however, she just wanted me to sit with her, hold her hand and not say a word. From time to time she'd smile or wink at me, happy, contented and completely at peace. She would not allow me to leave until one of the nurses reminded me that visiting hours were over.

The following day, when I walked in alone, Sze Sze looked at the door as if to ask, Isn't Ena coming? I told her, "Ena is still feeling quite miserable; I'm afraid you may have to do without her a few more days and just put up with this old man." When I had time to sit with her and relax, she indicated she wanted me to talk, so I began, "Do you feel you are getting better, Sze Sze?"

Yes.

"Wonderful! I'm very grateful for that. For quite a long time, you were a very sick young woman, Sze Sze. Auntie Ena and I were very worried about you. We phoned the home almost every day, sometimes twice a day, to find out how you were doing, and the news wasn't very good. I was quite upset, at times, and sad—do you think it is alright for a man to cry?"

She didn't know.

"Well, sometimes I did. There were times I thought I might not see you again before getting to heaven. Do you know what I found the most difficult at that time? You were so far away. I could not be with you; I couldn't ask what you wanted me to pray for."

Her eyes asked for an explanation of that last statement.

"What I mean is . . . I didn't know what you wanted. Did you want to get better or did you want to die. The Aunties asked us to pray for your recovery—I can understand that—and for myself, I also wanted you to get better. There were times, however, when I wondered if I was being selfish . . . what I wondered about was what you wanted. Do you now understand what I mean?"

Her eyes told me she did.

"Now, if you let me, I want to ask some personal questions," I continued. "Remember, you do not have to answer them if you think I have no right to ask them." I looked at her eyes. They told me it was okay, so I asked, "Did you think you were going to die?"

Yes.

"Were you afraid to die?"

She smiled but kept her tongue.

"Now, tell me Sze Sze . . . did you want to die?"

Her tongue came out, slowly, and tears began to fill her eyes. I held her hand. She wept softly. I wondered what was going through her mind. What was she thinking? Did my questions make her realize that by now she could have been freed from the body that had held her hostage most of her life?

I let her weep a while. Then I asked, "Now that you are getting better, are you happy?"

She smiled through her tears.

"What do you think, Sze Sze, have these last few months changed you? Has what has happened to you drawn you closer to God, made you a stronger Christian?"

She smiled again.

I dried her tears. We were quiet for some time, enjoying each other's presence. Then she began to cry again. It was a different kind of crying that had nothing to do with sadness or strong emotions. "Are you in pain? Do you want me to call a nurse?"

Yes.

By now, visiting hours were almost over. It was time for me to leave. I wished her a good night and told her I would talk to one of the nurses. As I passed by the nurses' station, I told the nurse on duty that Sze Sze was in pain. She replied it was time to administer another dose of pain medication and got up.

The following day Ena was still battling her cold, so, again, I made the journey to the hospital alone. I found a discouraged Sze Sze, disheartened by the slow rate of recovery. She didn't want me to talk, and I didn't know what to do to cheer her. We just sat there, both engrossed in our own thoughts. Suddenly I saw her face light up, and she began to bounce on her mattress. I followed the direction of her eyes and saw Jacqueline Au Yeung enter the ward. When I got up to give them an opportunity to spend time together, Jacqueline insisted I stay. Soon an animated Jacqueline began to rattle rapidly in Cantonese and had Sze Sze giggling constantly. Before she left, we sang some hymns and choruses.

After Jacqueline left, Sze Sze and I had some time together. Jacqueline's visit had done my friend a world of good, left her in high spirits and put her in a teasing mood. When the time came for me to leave, I asked, as I did most evenings, "Do you want to see this old man again tomorrow?"

She held her tongue.

I wasn't sure whether she was still teasing or serious, so I asked, "Do you want a visit tomorrow?"

Yes.

"Do you know of anyone who is coming tomorrow?"

Yes.

"Mom?"

No.

"Your brother?"

Her answer was a big smile. "Wonderful, that will give me my first day off since coming to Hong Kong."

It was good to have the day off. It gave me an opportunity to spend extra time with Dibs, Shaan and the other members of the family. I usually see Dibs off to the center in the morning and give Shaan and the others rides during the day if the weather is not too cold, but by the time we return from the hospital, they are all sound asleep. Now I was there to welcome Dibs home from the center, feed her and do devotions with her and the others. They all needed the extra attention; they all felt I had neglected them.

After my morning coffee, I dropped in at the office to get paper for my printer. Uncle Pete asked, "How's Sze Sze doing?"

"Making small gains most days, but there are days she still suffers a lot of pain. Sometimes she's discouraged by the slow progress she is making. It must seem to her she's been in that hospital forever."

"I'm quite angry with God," he burst out. "I can accept that He has so his purposes with Sze Sze—whatever they may be. But why take a beautiful girl—one who was born perfectly normal and allow her to become physically handicapped—one who has already suffered so much, and then make her suffer so much more. I don't seem to understand him at all."

"Well, Pete, I've asked myself the same questions more than once. Unfortunately, I haven't been able to come up with any acceptable answers. I have simply learned to trust that He knows what He is doing. One thing I know for sure, He doesn't owe you or me or anyone else an explanation of his actions."

The following day Ena decided she had coddled her cold long enough and accompanied me again on my visit to the hospital. When she entered the hospital, she donned a mask to be on the safe side. Sze Sze welcomed us with a weak smile. She told us she was experiencing pain again, but looking at her eyes, I felt that there was more. Perhaps there was something else bothering her. What it was became apparent when Ena asked, "Did you have a nice visit with your brother yesterday?"

Her face fell.

"Do you mean he didn't show up?"

Yes.

I made up my mind to ignore Sze Sze the next time she told us not to visit. It is possible, of course, she had misunderstood when her brother would come to visit, because a few minutes before the end of visiting hours he dropped in, giving him, perhaps, ten minutes with his sister—not long enough for us to stay away.

Apart from our visits, Sze Sze received little attention, other than the ministrations of doctors and nurses. It isn't that she or any other member of the family who needs to be hospitalized is neglected by the home. They are visited each day by one of the care givers, putting a strain on the often understaffed household. Our daily visits to the hospital helped relieve that problem.

Staff at Prince of Wales, both doctors and nurses, was very approachable. Maybe because we spent so much time with Sze Sze, they were always willing to answer questions. During one of our visits, a doctor came to examine her. He asked us to go to the waiting area until he had completed his bedside visit. After we were allowed in again, I asked, "How is Sze Sze doing, doctor, is she making any real progress?"

Sze Sze, My Daughter

He sat down on one of the vacant chairs, crossed his legs, put down his clipboard and began, "Yes, she is, but very slowly. Her stomach and intestines have been inactive for about two months now. They need to resume their regular functions—they have to be restarted, so to speak—and that will take time. All this time she has been fed intravenously, but recently we have started to feed her partly through the gastrostomy. That is progress."

"Do you think she will be able to come home for the Chinese New Year?"

"I think that's highly unlikely. As long as she is unable to take food by mouth, she won't go home."

"Thank you, doctor," I said, "I understand, but it will be quite a disappointment for her and us to have her miss both Christmas and the Chinese New Year." The doctor picked up is clipboard and got up, and we walked back to the ward.

While Ena refreshed Sze Sze's face and vaselined her lips, I asked our young friend when she'd had her last bed bath? She couldn't remember. Hospital care in Hong Kong is different in many ways from that in Canada. Nurses do not bathe patients who need help; family and friends take care of this. During visiting hours, you can see visitors scurry back and forth between bathroom and patients, carry basins of water, soap, wash cloths and towels, and bathe their loved ones. From time to time, one of the care givers of the home visited Sze Sze, usually outside visiting hours, and gave her a good scrubbing.

Just before we left for home, I remembered that a friend had offered a number of cassette tapes with sermons preached in Cantonese. When I asked Sze Sze if she would like to listen to them, her face brightened. "I know you have a portable disc player," I said, "but do you also have a cassette player?"

No.

"Well, then we will have to find one. Do you also want us to bring your Walkman and CDs?"

She smiled and her tongue came out. On the way home, we dropped in at Broadway Electronics at the Landmark Shopping Center to buy a cassette player.

The following morning I reported to Wendy on Sze Sze's progress. I talked about her ups and downs and related my conversation with the doctor. I also expressed my concern about Sze Sze's seating arrangement. "Someone dragged Sau Ming's old recliner chair

Sze Sze, My Daughter

to the hospital," I said. "Sze Sze is very uncomfortable in it; it simply isn't suitable for her."

"I'm glad you told me about this. I'll discuss this with Pui Yee. We should be able to do better," she replied. "This afternoon I have to be in Shatin, not too far from the hospital. Perhaps I should drop in at Sze Sze's and have a look at it myself. Is there anything else I should know about?"

"Yes, Sze Sze can't remember when she's had her last bed bath. I'm sure she would appreciate a good scrubbing. Would it be alright for Ena to give her one?"

"By all means, if she feels comfortable doing it. Have her talk to Pui Yee. She will give her all the things she needs to give Sze Sze a bath."

When I talked to Pui Yee about the bed bath and asked her to get ready all the needed supplies, she felt this would be too much for Ena. She sounded almost defensive when she declared, "Don't worry, Uncle Bill, I will take care of it. I don't want Auntie Ena to have to do this."

That afternoon, while we were waiting at the gate for the bus, Pui Yee hailed us. She offered to give us a lift to the hospital. On the back seat of the van she had a large bag bulging with stuff. We arrived at the hospital about half an hour early. Before taking the elevator to Ward 3E, we had a cup of coffee at the canteen. When we got to the ward, I asked Pui Yee, "Do you want me to draw the curtains around Sze Sze's bed for you to give her a bath?"

She breezed, "No need to do that, Uncle Bill. I'll just wash her face, arms and legs." We felt frustrated. These were the things we did for her every day. What Sze Sze needed was to have her body washed thoroughly.

After Pui Yee had left, we unloaded our bag on Sze Sze's bed: a cassette player and sermon tapes and her Walkman and CD's. Holding up the cassette player in one hand and the disc player in the other, I asked, "Tell me, young lady, which do want to listen to first, a sermon or some pop music?"

She fastened her eyes on the Walkman. "Okay, my friend, music it will be," I laughed. "Choose a disc." She picked one. I popped it into the player, placed an ear bud into her left ear—she doesn't hear well with her right ear—adjusted the volume and watched her wiggle and giggle with delight. Just before we were about to leave, she indicated she wanted to listen to a sermon. She chose one and I put it in the player. I pushed the play button and adjusted the sound level. We then wished her a good night and left her to listen to the tape.

The following morning, just when we were about to leave for church, Pui Yee stopped us and asked, "Uncle Bill, would you have a look at this recliner. I want you to fix two boards to it, one on each side? It will keep Sze Sze from falling off. I want to take it to the hospital this afternoon."

"I'm sorry, Pui Yee, we are on our way to church now," I replied. "Besides, it is rather difficult to nail a wooden board to a tubular, aluminum frame." Now, Pui Yee is nothing if not persistent and persuasive. She kept coming at me with other suggestions, none of them very practical, to keep Sze Sze from falling off that recliner. By the time we were able to break free from her without becoming rude, we had missed our bus. The next two didn't stop because they were full, so were forced to hail a taxi to get to church.

When we came home from church, we found that Auntie Wendy had sewn a harness to hold Sze Sze in place on the recliner. Later that afternoon, when we arrived at the hospital, we found our friend sitting triumphant and relaxed on the recliner. Auntie Wendy had given her not only a safe and more comfortable way of sitting but also a good scrubbing. She had taken Sau Ming's old chair with her when she left for home.

When we asked Sze Sze how she felt, she indicated that she felt not much different from the last few days. Later, while she was listening to hymns on her Walkman, she directed me with her eyes to her communication board. She wanted to tell us something. I slid my finger down the subject list: *I* . . . .

Yes.

I moved to the next list: *am . . . have . . . want to . . . feel* . . . .

Yes.

Next I moved to: *happy . . . sad . . . anxious* . . . .

Yes.

I looked at her and said, "You feel anxious about something. What is it you feel anxious about, Sze Sze, that you won't get better?"

No.

"Because it takes so long—are you discouraged about the slowness of the healing process?"

Yes.

"Do you want me to pray with you; shall we ask God to give patience and to take away your anxiety?"

Yes. Before Ena and I left for home, we had a time of prayer together.

And so, day followed day. Visit followed visit. We made our daily trek to the hospital, spent time with our friend, watched her slow progress and made our way home again. She was now in her eleventh week of hospitalization. Each visit took a four-hour bite out of our day, took us away from involvement with other members of the family and slowed down whatever building or maintenance projects I was involved in. But realizing how long the days for Sze Sze must be and how much our visits meant to her, we gladly made our daily visit. Being emotionally involved in Sze Sze's life, however, took its toll on me. At first I did not realize how much, but one day, when Sze Sze was once again running a high fever and showing discouragement, it hit me. I wondered how much longer she needed to be in hospital and went home quite disheartened. The following morning in chapel, in the middle of my prayer for a miracle, I broke down. I found it difficult to continue.

It was sunny but crisp on the last day of the Year of the Monkey. All over Hong Kong, flower markets had sprung up and blossomed. Potted mini orange trees competed with flowers of various shapes and colors for the attention of last-minute shoppers, browsers looking for the perfect, flowering plum branch or flawless orchid to help usher in the Year of the Rooster. This is the time of year Pui Yee traditionally organizes for the family outings to those markets. This year was no exception. Care givers bundled up the kids and Kit bused them in shifts to Sheung Shui, to a sports field that had been converted to flower market. Being surrounded by crowds of people and a riot of colors brought joy to their faces. Even those who could not see showed excitement, sensing different sounds and smells. It was interesting to observe the reaction of shoppers to the large influx of severely handicapped people. A few looked at them with obvious disgust. They spoiled their shopping pleasure and marred the esthetic experience of shopping for splendor. Others stopped to talk to the kids. They held up flowers for them to see or smell, or they gave them a bud or blossom.

I spent some time at stalls selling decorations, choosing some to cheer up Sze Sze's corner of the ward. That afternoon we were greeted by a cheerful Sze Sze. Her fever was gone and she looked good. When I unpacked the decorations and assembled them, she showed great excitement. It was when I was ready to hang banners

Sze Sze, My Daughter

with New Year's blessings and a red, paper lantern on her IV stand, that I discovered she was no longer on intravenous feeding.

"Hey!" I exclaimed, "What happened to your drip? It's gone!"

She beamed.

I looked at her radiant face. Something else was different . . . but what? Then it dawned on me. The drain tube had been removed from her nose. "Well—I'll be—your tube's gone too!"

Another broad smile. Sze Sze then directed Ena's attention to her night stand. It was cluttered with a pack of nappies, a jar of Vaseline, a box of cotton swabs, some wet wipes and a thermos flask.

Ena went down the list, "Do you want me to wipe your face?"

No.

"Clean your nose?"

No.

"Grease your lips?"

No.

Looking at the thermos, Ena asked, "Water?"

A large grin and her tongue told Ena that was what she wanted.

I turned to point at the sign above Sze Sze's bed to caution Ena, "You can't because—uh—what—the 'nil by mouth' sign has disappeared!" I exclaimed. It had been replaced by another, written in Chinese characters only. I recognized enough of them to decipher that she was allowed small sips of water. To be on the safe side, I checked with one of the nurses, and she showed me a syringe which we were to use. Sze Sze was allowed 5 to 10 cc per serving. It was a joy to see Sze Sze's face when Ena squirted some water into her mouth.

We were overjoyed!

It was New Year's Eve. Visiting hours had been extended, so we stayed one hour longer to help Sze Sze celebrate. Just when we were about to leave, Pui Yee dropped in to see how Sze Sze was doing and to give her a bath. Ena and I waited in the canteen for Pui Yee to finish. As we walked to the parking lot with Pui Yee, my heart overflowed with gratitude. That morning I had asked for a miracle, and God had answered my prayer. It was wonderful to see the overnight change in our young friend.

On New Year's Day, Sze Sze was full of energy and mischief. She was clutching a small, stuffed animal, a dog, when we came to her bedside. Ena asked, "What is the name of your pooch, Sze Sze?"

"Bll," she blurted and laughed hilariously. She knows that I was born in the Year of the Dog.

Sze Sze, My Daughter

"Oh, you rat!" I exclaimed in mock indignation. Sze Sze was born in the Year of the Rat. I think that was when I started to call her Rattekin at times.

On the first Thursday of the new year, we had a wonderful recording session in chapel. Junko had come to sing and play with the family, and Pui Yee suggested we record our joyful noise. We played and sang and had much fun doing it. Dib Dib was in top form. She is always noisy and full of fun, but come singing time, she becomes serious, producing a steady and monotonous bwah-wah bwah-wah bwah-wah. When I told her how much Sze Sze would enjoy her singing, she beamed with pride and crowed with delight. Pui Yee went around with the mike and got it all on tape: Dib Dib's Bwah-wahs, Shaan Shaan's kai-kai-ahs, Ping Pong's giggles, Anna's occasional strum on her guitar and Wing Kit's a-rhythmic banging his toy.

It was on a sunny and mild day in the second week of February that Ena and I decided to go to the hospital at three rather than four-thirty; we were hoping the nurses would let us enter the ward. They did. Sze Sze was on her recliner, held neatly in place by the harness Wendy had sewn. We asked one of the nurses if we could take Sze Sze down to the garden. She thought it would be a marvelous idea to give her some fresh air after having been inside for more than two months. She undid the gastrostomy tube and covered Sze Sze with a blanket. We took with us a bottle of water and a small, plastic cup for our friend and set off on our outing. The elevator brought us down to the ground floor level, and we ambled to the canteen to get some coffee-to-go. Then we headed for the garden and sat down on one of the benches in a covered area. After having been confined to the ward for so many weeks, Sze Sze was delighted to be outside. We told her we had a surprise for her. Not knowing what to expect, she looked with anticipation as we popped a tape into her cassette player. I put an ear bud into her ear, hit the play button and watched her reaction. Soon she started to chuckle and giggle; then her eyes got moist. "You miss the other kids, don't you?" Ena asked.

Yes.

"They miss you too. That's why they made this tape for you."

After a while she began to show signs of fatigue and wanted to go back to the ward. There the nurses transferred her to her bed. By the time we had packed our bag, she was almost asleep, a smile on her face. We were back in time for supper with the rest of the staff.

This was only the second time since our return to the home that this had happened.

When we visited Sze Sze the following day, we discovered she had reached another mile stone. She was allowed a thin gruel, another sign she was well on her way to full recovery. One of the nurses told us that if her body would tolerate this semi-solid food and process it properly, it would not be long before she could go home.

We continued to visit Sze Sze outside regular visiting hours. The nurses were cooperative. They usually had her securely strapped on her recliner, the gastrostomy tube disconnected or willing to unplug it if it wasn't—she would be ready for a trip to the garden on mild days or, on colder days, for a ride down the many corridors, the canteen or the main lobby of the hospital. Going to visit early meant coming home early, having supper with the rest of the staff and doing devotions with the family after they had gone to bed.

One sunny day, when we came to the hospital, she was waiting for us to take her for a ride to the garden. Before we wheeled her off, I stopped to check if her tube had been disconnected. There was none. Her gastrostomy had been removed. It was the last of the life lines—vessels pumping food and medicine into her body and tubes carrying wastes out—that had been removed. She was completely fed by mouth now and on a soft diet. If no complications developed, she would soon be going home.

We took Sze Sze to the garden and sat on one of the stone benches in the colonnade. She was in a mischievous mood. While I was giving her a drink, squeezing Ribena juice from a plastic pouch, squirting it through a tube into her mouth, her left hand suddenly swung around, grasped the pouch and squashed it. The result was disastrous. The deep purple juice splashed all over her face and blanket, and Ena's jacket and my slacks were covered with the plum-colored liquid. She burst out laughing and found it difficult to stop. Considering that both her gross and fine motor movements are mostly involuntary and uncoordinated, it was an extraordinary feat for her to grasp and squeeze the pouch. She was very naughty all through the visit, showing she was rapidly becoming the old Sze Sze again.

At the home they were making preparations for Sze Sze's homecoming. They had received word her discharge from the hospital was imminent. Her bed was moved from the small to the large bedroom, the room where those who need constant supervision live, and the place where the nurse in charge has her desk.

Sze Sze, My Daughter

The long awaited call came on the morning of February 17, a day full of sunshine and brimming with promise. Sze Sze was at last ready to come home; her long ordeal had finally come to an end. At about ten-thirty, Wendy, Ena and I boarded the bus to collect her from Prince of Wales Hospital, her home for almost three months. While Wendy and Ena tidied her up and packed her belongings, I went down to the canteen, savoring one more time a cup of brew in the place that had become so familiar, hoping I would never need to visit it again. When I returned to the ward, I was just in time to help Wendy transfer Sze Sze from the bed to the recliner. We were now ready for the journey home. Wendy wheeled the recliner toward the door, and Ena and I carried bags with Sze Sze's belongings. We were ready to leave the ward. The nurses on duty were lined up along the passage way, bidding Sze Sze farewell and wishing her good luck. It was a royal send off for a brave young woman. We rode down the elevator to the bus where Kit Chow was waiting. He opened the back of the bus, lowered the lift and rolled the recliner onto it, all the while chatting cheerily to Sze Sze. Once she was inside the bus, he carefully secured the recliner and started the bus. Sze Sze was finally on her way home.

As we rode home, it was wonderful to watch the joy and excitement mount on her thin face. She craned her neck to drink in the scenery. As we came closer to home, the sights became more and more familiar, and her excitement increased. At the home she was welcomed with cheers and hugs. Then she was trundled off to have a real bath, her first in three months.

In the afternoon, after her nap, I took Sze Sze for a ride in the garden where we made our familiar loop. We stopped at the barbeque pit, the spot where we had shared so many special moments in the past. For a while we just sat there, enjoying the quiet, the flowers and each other's company. After a while she looked at me, smiled and rolled up her eyes. They filled with tears as I offered a prayer of thanksgiving.

Chapter 11

Sze Sze's first night at home had been uncomfortable; she had experienced pain and felt discouraged. I grabbed one of the red, plastic stools that are found all around the home and placed it beside her bed. I took her hand and began, "Listen, dear friend, just because you are no longer in hospital doesn't mean that you are completely better. It does mean that you are no longer so ill that you need to be cared for by doctors and nurses. But, you know, there is still a lot of healing that has to happen inside your body. For almost three months, you were fed intravenously. Now your insides will have to get used to processing more solid food, stuff that enters your body the normal way, through your mouth and stomach. You are still very weak and need to get stronger. You will have to put on pounds, because you are as skinny as a rat, my Rattekin. There will be more days and nights that you will feel discomfort." Her dark eyes, large in her thin face, locked into mine and clouded over. "But you know what," I concluded, "I can assure you that healing will go much faster because you are at home now. You are surrounded by the loving care of the family, and that will make all the difference." That brought a thin smile to her face.

It was wonderful for Ena and me that we no longer needed to make our daily hospital visits. We settled into a regular routine of giving rides to the kids, playing games with them and helping them at meal times. I was able to take on a number of maintenance jobs and started some small building projects. Ena and I also resumed our rounds in the bedrooms to do devotions with the family. In the hospital I had finished reading with Sze Sze the devotions I had written on Psalm 23, and I wondered how she would take to my reflections on the Book of Romans, a series I had begun at her request. Would she like them? Would they be too deep for her? I need not have worried. She showed a great deal of interest, and she responded well to my questions. Her choice of Romans for Bible study, her interest in the lessons and her understanding of the

Sze Sze, My Daughter

subject matter were evidence of her spiritual hunger and an indication of her intelligence.

Because we spent more of our time in the home, we had an opportunity to get re-acquainted with the other family members and get to know them better. Take Fa Fa, for instance. This teenager, by far the most photogenic member of the family, had been abandoned by her parents when she was a baby. She had been found with severe burns on arms and legs after a Chinese New Year's celebration. Medication for epileptic seizures dulls her understanding of what is happening in the world around her, and she is unable to walk, talk or feed herself. What she can do is smile. She does so generously—whoever approaches her is blessed with a most dazzling smile.

When Fa Fa returned home from Pine Hill Village School the first school day after the New Year's break, she was welcomed by Mindy, one of our regular volunteers. She removed Fa Fa's schoolbag from the handles of her wheelchair and the splints from her legs, placed them on a shelf and started to feed Fa Fa her evening meal. When she spotted me, she gave me one of her radiant smiles. I walked up to her and asked—not expecting an appropriate response—"Hi, my beautiful flower[14], did you enjoy being back at school?"

She smiled and vigorously shook her head.

Surprised I laughed, "O, you would have liked another holiday!"

This time she nodded and laughed.

"Ah . . . I think you are a bit lazy . . . right!"

Again she nodded.

"Perhaps also naughty?"

This time she shook her head.

"No, Uncle Bill," Mindy interjected, "I think Fa Fa is cheeky."

This time she again bobbed her head and laughed loudly.

I was amazed. Never before had I received such appropriate responses from our young friend. I had often wondered how much understanding was hiding behind all those wonderful smiles. This incident made me move up my evaluation of her intelligence a notch or two. It also reminded me to be careful to speak to our children rather than about them in their presence, thinking they will not understand.

It was flu season. Centers and schools for special needs children were closed. After the SARS epidemic of 2003, the health authorities in Hong Kong have become very proactive in preventing the spread of infectious diseases, especially among the most vulnerable, the elderly and those with special needs. Several members of the family were affected, causing them to run a high fever and cough. Pui Yee was on a two-week vacation in England, and Pat, who was now in charge, set the small bedroom apart as isolation ward. All care givers were ordered to wear masks and use latex gloves to prevent spreading the flu to those who were healthy. Visitors were not allowed in the isolation ward. I wondered how soon Sze Sze would catch whatever bug it was that made the family ill, for, I supposed, her natural resistance to infections had been killed by all the antibiotics she had been given during her stay in hospital.

One day while I was feeding Sze Sze, she coughed in my face. I wiped the food off my glasses and asked, "Sze Sze, the next time you feel a cough coming, would you please turn your head? I know you can't cover your coughs, but I'm sure you can turn your head." A little later she again coughed in my face and thought it was funny. I finished feeding her, brought her to her bedroom and said, "Miss Chan, you know I love you, but I want you to know I do not love all the things you do. Coughing deliberately in my face is one of those things."

After her nap, Sze Sze spent time with us in our flat. She kept eyeing me, trying to gauge my mood. I looked at her and said, "I guess that you notice I'm disappointed with you." She acknowledged my supposition. "You know, young lady, what you did when I fed you—coughing intentionally in my face—was not only rude but also, especially at a time when so many of the family are sick with flu, a very unhealthy thing to do. I don't know what made you cough—food going down the wrong way or a cold—whatever it was, I didn't appreciate you doing it in my face. The next time you cough in my face on purpose, I will ask someone else to feed you. Is that clear?"

She looked at me with audacity and stuck out her tongue.

When the evening meal was served, she didn't want me to feed her. The following day Sze Sze was brought to the isolation ward. She had a high fever, a runny nose and a nasty cough. Whenever I made my appearance, masked and gloved, to help feed the family, she wanted to be fed by anyone but me. The days wore on; her attitude did not change. When I talked with her, she either ignored me or made replies meant to hurt me. She was hiding a hurt she couldn't or wouldn't express. All I could do was show I cared for her and wait until she was ready to talk.

Life on the isolation ward was a drag. Only people who cared for the sick were allowed to visit; casual visitors were kept out. To break the monotony for the patients, Ena and I put on a puppet show. After the show, I asked Sze Sze if she found life on the ward boring. She didn't.

"Don't you miss hanging out with Dibs and Shaan, Auntie Ena and me in our flat?" I asked.

No.

"You would rather be here than in our cozy kitchen?"

She faced me, looked at me provocatively and showed me the back end of her tongue.

"Well, my friend," I answered, "let me not spoil your pleasure. I'm going to make myself a cup of coffee. I'll be back. Let me know when you are ready to talk." I then left her.

Dealing with Sze Sze's behavior made me realize how we all, at times, when we are hurting deeply, take out our frustrations on those we love the most. We test the limits of their tolerance and endurance, knowing they will understand we are suffering and trusting they will help us deal with our pain when we are ready to let them. Being assured of their affection, we test the depth of their love and know that, in the end, we will be forgiven by them. This is true of us who can put our pain into words; how much more of those who can't, who must act out their suffering or wait for others to ferret it out of them.

Sze Sze was once again going through a period of loneliness. Since her discharge from the hospital almost one month earlier, she had received no attention from her mother or brother. What she really needed more than anything else was something I couldn't give her: the companionship of someone her own age.

It took a while for Sze Sze to emerge from her struggle with whatever demons beset her. It came in stages: after she had been discharged from the isolation ward, she slowly began to take an interest in her surroundings again; next, she allowed me once more to feed her; finally, the indifference she had shown at devotion time slowly vanished. She became hungry for spiritual nourishment again.

Although Ena and I did not often venture out in the evening, there were days we did not have time to do devotions with the family. One evening—we had been invited for dinner by friends—we went to the bedrooms to wish the family a quick goodnight. We didn't want them to wait for us in vain. As we went from bed to bed, Sze Sze followed us with her eyes. At Fa Fa's bed I sang a short prayer. When I turned around, I noticed Sze Sze's intent gaze on me. I stopped at her bed and said, "I seldom sing to you, do I? Do you want me to sing for you?"

Yes.

"Your favorite song?"

A hesitant yes.

"How about our special version of your favorite song?"

Now a smile spread across her face. I grabbed a stool, lowered the bedrail and sat down. Sze Sze laid her cheek on my arm, and I began, "Give thanks with a grateful heart, Give thanks to the Holy One, Give thanks He's given Sze Sze as my special friend . . . ." Usually this produces a warm smile. This time I felt tears trickle on my arm. I gave her a hug and a kiss and wished her sweet dreams. Now I knew our relationship was fully restored. I breathed a quick prayer of thanks, as I rushed out to the car park where our friends were waiting for me. I joined Ena who was already seated in the back of the car.

Before Sze Sze would be allowed to go back to the center, it was important for her to be able to sit for long periods of time in her wheelchair. Therefore, Wendy ordered staff to put Sze Sze in her chair, first, for one hour and gradually for longer periods of time. At first they complied with the order, but after a while they became careless and left her on her recliner, hoping her work would keep Wendy busy in the office. They found it easier to walk with Wai Ching in the garden, than have two people spend fifteen minutes to get Sze Sze in her chair and then have to reverse the process an hour or so later. From time to time, they needed a reminder, that they had been hired to serve the family, and that the family was not there to give them a convenient job.

Caring for Sze Sze is labor intensive. Lifting her from bed or recliner and placing her into her wheelchair requires two workers, three when she is not fully relaxed. Securing her in her chair takes two people fifteen minutes. They need to lower her on the specially molded seat, strap her across each thigh to the seat and around the waist to the back of the chair. Next they must place a soft plastic shield across her chest. Its bottom straps keep her torso firmly tied to the back of the chair; its upper straps hold in place the neck brace, cross her shoulders and keep them securely against the back of the chair. Then they need to adjust the headrest, snap in place the side supports to keep her from sagging sideways, put on the leg splints and secure them to the footrests and, finally, slide in place the tray with its posts allowing her to steady herself.

Sze Sze, My Daughter

For Sze Sze's comfort, it is important that she is properly positioned on the seat before all the securing is done, that all the straps are fixed in the correct places and that all restraints are tightened just right—too tight or too loose is equally uncomfortable for her. Once she has been secured in her chair, she will be in it for many hours, unable to shift her position, adjust her restraints or voice her discomfort. Unfortunately, she is not always secured in her chair by the same care givers, and all are not as careful and attentive to her needs as they should be. Some are chatting constantly without checking with Sze Sze to see if what they are doing is done correctly. Sometimes, after I collected her from the Play Room, she would direct me with her eyes to parts of her webbing that were not done up properly. Generally, her headrest had been dropped into its slot but not tightened; often, one or both shoulder straps, holding in place her neck brace, had been fastened too tight or not tight enough; occasionally, one of the lower straps of the plastic shield had not been secured.

One sunny afternoon, we took Sze Sze and Dibs for a long walk. We allowed Sze Sze to lead the way. She directed us past the soccer pitch across the road from the home to the overpass crossing the highway. Then she guided us past the Kwu Tung Market and into the countryside. Both girls were delighted to venture away from the home and into different surroundings. As days and weeks passed, we noticed a change in Sze Sze; she was regaining her strength, showed signs she was happy to be alive and appeared to be at peace and content.

The Home of Loving Faithfulness has a way of working itself into the hearts of those who visit it or volunteer there. It attracts volunteers from countries all over the world, and sooner or later they feel a tug at their hearts' strings to revisit the home. One such person was Evelyn, a young woman from Switzerland, who had volunteered at the home six years earlier. She was vacationing in Asia and spent part of her time with the family. With Ena she took some of the kids on shopping trips to New Town Plaza in Sha Tin. I considered these all-girls' outings, so I decided to stay home and devote my time to doing maintenance projects. Shaan Shaan and Fung Tai were the first who were taken on such a shopping excursion. The following day they took Dibs and bought her a game for her birthday. Sze Sze was last. She took some of her own money, just in case.

This was her first big outing. I wondered how well she would last sitting in her chair for about four hours. When she returned, she seemed none the worse for wear. "Show me the things on which you've spent all your money," I demanded. She hadn't spent a penny. "O, you tightwad," I teased. "Tell me, did you enjoy your trip to New Town Plaza?"

Yes.

"Wasn't it special to go on an all-girls' outing?"

She looked at me thoughtfully, waited and answered no.

"Ah, you would have liked it better if this old Billy goat had come along?"

She laughed and stuck out her tongue.

"You flatterer—you sure have a way of making an old man feel young again!" I guffawed.

Sze Sze loves to play games, and she had discovered a new one she liked, Connect Four. It was the game Dibs had received for her birthday. It is a strategy game played by two players. Each player chooses a color, red or yellow. They take turns sliding one disk at a time of the color they have chosen into one of seven parallel slots. The first person who forms a series of four consecutive disks of the same color, horizontally, vertically or diagonally, wins the game. It didn't take Sze Sze long to become good at it. At game time, Ena and I played taking turns with Dibs, Shaan and Sze Sze. The first two had little idea of what they are doing, but they enjoyed the interaction with us. Sze Sze, however, played to win, and she often did.

There is a bit of rivalry between Dibs and Sze Sze. Both vie for my attention in the mainly female world of the Home of Loving Faithfulness. Although I try to pay attention to Dibs and Shaan as well as Sze Sze, Dibs, at times, is jealous of Sze Sze. One Sunday afternoon, after I had played a number of games with Dib Dib and Shaan, I asked Dibs, "May I now play a game with Sze Sze?"

Dibs's hand did not go up.

"Are you telling me that Sze Sze is not allowed to play with your game?"

This time she scowled and her hand shot up.

I turned to Sze Sze and said, "Sorry, my friend, we better play another game." She looked at Dibs as if to say, "I don't need your game," and chose to play SKIP BO instead. From that time on, she no longer asked to play Connect Four.

The time had come to celebrate Sze Sze's Christmas party. When she was so very ill at Christmas, she had been promised a private Christmas party when she came home again. With Auntie Val and Sze Sze, we settled on Monday, March 21. I looked at our friend and teased, "You don't expect a Christmas present from Auntie Ena and me, do you? It's almost Easter."

She looked at me as if to say, "Are you kidding? Of course I expect a present."

"Give us an idea of what you have in mind . . . *clothes* . . . a *CD* . . . a *DVD* . . . a *game* . . . ."

Yes.

Although I had a suspicion of what she wanted, I asked, "What kind of game?"

Sze Sze promptly turned her head and looked straight at the cupboard that held Dibs's game. "Ah, I understand," I said. "You do not want to be at the mercy of your friend Dibs."

She acknowledged my suspicion with a knowing look.

And so, in the same week we celebrated Good Friday, we had Sze Sze's Christmas party. In addition to Sze Sze's presents, Auntie Val had bought small gifts for Dibs, Shaan and Fung Tai, to make them feel included. When Sze Sze tore the wrapping off the present Ena and I had bought for her, she cast a triumphant look at Dibs.

Shortly after celebrating Sze Sze's party, we experienced a crisis of sorts in the home. Auntie Val was hospitalized and admitted to intensive care at Nethersole Hospital. It all began with a fall. At the time, she was taking care of the children on the upper deck of the Ark, while Uncle Pete and Auntie Sue were vacationing in England. She had stepped on a toy, which caused her to sprain her knee. That didn't do much to slow her down. She moved around the home in a wheelchair, doing the things she normally does, checking and ordering supplies, making sure guestrooms were ready for expected visitors and staying in touch with friends of the home worldwide.

Then she caught a cold, which turned into a bronchial infection, which, in turn, deteriorated into pneumonia in both her lungs—I guess that forty years of tirelessly giving of herself had finally caught up with her. We were all very concerned. E-mails went out, and people all over the world were praying for her recovery. At first, she wasn't doing well. It almost seemed as if she had lost the will to fight. Doctors were trying hard to identify the virus that had laid her low. Heavy doses of medication helped her pull through. She began to show some improvement and was placed on an open ward. When she finally came home, she had aged considerably;

her body was at home, but her spirit hadn't caught up with it. It took quite a while for Auntie Val to regain her strength and spirit.

In the hot and humid climate of Hong Kong, paint jobs do not last long. Plaster on the concrete walls of the home needs to be well-sealed before it can be painted. As soon as moisture penetrates the seal, walls and ceilings begin to blister, and rooms take on a battered look. The bedrooms in the C Block had reached that state of dilapidation and needed to be redone, causing quite an upheaval. The Play Room of the C Block and the living area of the Lower Ark became temporary bedrooms. Beds and chests of drawers had to be moved from the regular bed rooms and placed in the temporary sleeping quarters. Protective screens were placed in the makeshift dormitories to protect the privacy of the family. Curtains and pictures needed to be taken down from windows and walls and put into temporary storage. Workers, who claimed to be experienced in repairing blistered walls and resealing them, were hired to do the job. They promised the work would be done expertly and quickly, but days turned into weeks and the work did not progress as promised. What was done looked shoddy. Then, one day, the workers did not show up for work, nor the next day or the following days. The job was half finished. It was now up to our two chauffeurs, Kim and Kit, to complete the job. I set aside my projects and decided to help them.

While Kim and Kit worked on the walls, I concentrated my energies on the many closets. Starting in the small bedroom, I pried open doors that had been painted shut, removed door handles and kick plates, and gave them to Ena to remove the paint from them. I repainted the closets which had been covered with a chalky substance that was supposed to pass for satin finish. I then replaced the cleaned hardware on the doors, swept the floor and let the staff know that the room was ready for a thorough cleaning. After all this preparation, curtains and pictures could be hung and beds and chests of drawers could be moved back in.

Because Ena and I spent so much time working in the bedrooms in the morning, our kids felt neglected. Therefore we decided to take the afternoon off and relax with them. We took them for rides in the garden. Afterward we gathered them in the kitchen for snacks and games. When it was time for their evening meal, the Play Room was still in such a chaotic state, that we were asked to feed Shaan, Dibs and Sze Sze in the kitchen of the Ark. That sent Dibs into paroxysms of joy. She is so uncomplicated, and it takes so little to make her happy. While Ena fed Shaan and I took care of Dibs's needs, Sze Sze waited for her turn. After we had brought Shaan and Dibs to their bedroom, Sze Sze took her time to eat her bowl of food. When she had finished eating, and I had cleaned her face and wiped her tray, she indicated she wanted to play one more game of Connect Four before she let me sent her off to bed.

The following day I worked right through lunch time to finish painting the closets in the big bedroom. When I was done, I nuked the lunch Ena had set aside for me, ate it, took a shower and had a short nap. Again we spent the afternoon with the kids.

After spending time with the kids, giving them rides and playing games, I tried to gauge Sze Sze's interest in resuming her lessons. Although her energy level seemed about as high as it had been before she became ill, she claimed she didn't have enough of it. She bristled when I asked if she had become lazy.

This wasn't the first time I had broached the subject of getting back to our studies; I had mentioned it a number of times at devotions, without receiving a more positive answer. I found it difficult to determine how much pressure to put on her. When we started our reading program, we had experienced a lot of problems, but then we hit upon a method that worked for her. I still hoped we would experience a similar breakthrough in spelling. I tried to reason with her, and I talked to her about her disabilities and abilities. "Listen, Sze Sze, when you were a baby and lost the use of your hands, feet and voice, the Lord left you a beautiful mind. It enabled you to learn how to read. Don't you believe we may find a new, a better way of spelling, like we did in reading?" She wasn't convinced and felt the need to pray about it. This sounded reasonable and commendable, but the answer she was waiting for was slow in coming. When I asked her if she wanted to discontinue lessons altogether, her answer was a definite no. However, I wasn't sure if she genuinely wanted to learn to read and spell better or craved the extra attention she received when I taught her. We were at a bit of an impasse. I decided to let the matter rest a while.

Sze Sze did show a passion for getting back on her computer. I hoped that by getting her to work on it, she might take an interest in taking up spelling again, so I remarked, "It's been a long time since you worked on your computer. Would you like me to dust it off and start it up for you?"

She looked at me and her tongue came out readily.

Sze Sze, My Daughter

"Now, let's see, where did we put it the last time we used it." I couldn't remember. The last time I had Sze Sze work on it must have been in the fall of the previous year. Then it suddenly struck me. When I was searching high and low for other items that had been displaced during the upheaval caused by painting the bedrooms, I couldn't remember having seen her Compaq. I searched the Lower Ark and went with a fine-tooth comb through all its closets and cupboards, but I couldn't find it. Next I searched the C Block, without turning up the missing computer. When I asked Auntie Wendy and Uncle Pete, they couldn't remember having seen it, but they searched their offices nevertheless. Wherever we looked, Sze Sze's computer couldn't be found.

I was beginning to get a sinking feeling. Over the past few months, things had been disappearing from the home. It is a rather open place. Except for the doors of the offices and the dispensary when no one is working there, I cannot think of any other doors that are kept locked. The first one to report that something had disappeared from her room was Sandy, a Filipino domestic worker assisting Aunties Joan and Irena. She had reported her passport and Hong Kong ID card stolen. Then purses belonging to Auntie Wendy, Anna and Auntie Joan went missing. It usually happened during the day, when they were engaged elsewhere. It obviously was an inside job. Now I feared that, whoever was responsible for the disappearance of those items, may have helped herself to Sze Sze's computer.

I was quite upset about the disappearance of Sze Sze's computer. So was Sze Sze; she was heartbroken. I tried to comfort her, telling her that computers can be replaced. After a concerted search by the whole staff failed to produce the missing laptop, I started to look for a replacement computer. With the rapid development of ever more powerful laptops, I couldn't find anything with less than twenty gigabytes. One gig was more than sufficient for Sze Sze's needs. As I was wondering aloud about what to do, Ena suggested, "I've heard you mention that you want to upgrade to a more powerful toy, Bill. Why don't you buy yourself a new one and give your old one to Sze Sze." That sounded like a reasonable solution, so I backed up all my files, cleared my hard drive and prepared my computer for Sze Sze's use. After Uncle Pete had installed WiVik, I plugged in the tip switch. The program didn't respond. I called Doctor Eric at Polytech and explained to him my problem. "Let me see," he said, "I have time to see you tomorrow afternoon at . . . uh . . . four-thirty. Does that suit you? See me at

Sze Sze, My Daughter

the lab." When I arrived at the laboratory the following day, he was waiting for me. Together with one of his technicians, he rigged up a contraption that made the program work.

The next day I wanted to test the computer, but it refused to do what it was supposed to do, no matter what I tried. I called Polytech several times, but was unable to get a hold of either Doctor Eric or his assistant. Sze Sze was watching with great interest my futile attempts to get the computer to respond to the commands of the tip switch and Doctor Eric to answer my calls. When she noticed my rising level of frustration, she placed her hand on my arm. I looked at her, and she rolled up her eyes. "You want me to pray about this, don't you? You are right. I shouldn't wait with praying until all other means have failed." She smiled, and we had a word of prayer. Upon my *amen*, Uncle Pete walked in and asked how things were going. I told him about my fruitless efforts to make things work, and he answered, "Let me have a look at this beast," and he took the computer to his apartment. Half an hour later he brought it back to us. He had gotten it to work.

In the afternoon I wanted Sze Sze to try her new computer using the tip switch. She was seated in her recliner. Lately, sitting too long in her chair gave her severe pain in one of her hips. I taped the switch to her left lower arm, which rested by her side on the recliner. To activate the switch, all she needed to do was raise her fore arm about ninety degrees and let it drop again. The results were not exactly what I had hoped for; they were rather erratic, caused by a number of factors, some familiar, others unexpected. Among the familiar causes were timing and the inability to relax her muscles, keeping her arm from dropping back to the rest position. The unforeseen factors affecting the working of the switch involved movements of Sze Sze's fore arm other than going a neat ninety degrees straight up. Sometimes it rotated around its axis, at other times it swung outward from her body. All these unwanted movements interfered with the proper working of the tip switch.

It became clear that merely taping the switch to Sze Sze's arm would not do. I needed to design a device which would control the unwanted movements of her arm. I began to scrounge around storage rooms. They held an assortment of abandoned wheelchair parts and an intriguing variety of splints and prostheses. They had served different members of the family at one time or another.

One of the devices that caught my attention was a contraption that had once encased Sze Sze's pelvis after her hip operation.

Fleece-lined splints attached to it had kept her legs spread apart. At the hips those splints were attached to the pelvic harness by joints allowing for limited movement of her legs. Those joints could be calibrated to allow an exact range of movement. I was allowed to cannibalize this contraption to make a splint, a thingamabob which would eliminate, I hoped, all or some of the unwanted movements of Sze Sze's arm. I spent a day cutting the hard, resinous parts on either side of the joint. I then shaped them in boiling water to fit around Sze Sze's upper and lower arm, lined them with fleece and attached Velcro straps to keep them in place. When I placed the splint on her arm, it indeed controlled most of the unwanted movements, keeping her lower arm from turning around its axis and controlling most, but not all, of the outward swings.

The splint did not improve the problem of timing, nor did it help Sze Sze's arm return to the rest position after activating the switch. I had to go back to the drawing board. I figured that, if I would mount the tip switch on a lever that could be moved by pulling a string and be brought back to its initial position by means of a spring, I would be in business. The whole gadget could be held in place with suction cups. I could use as fulcrum one of the joints of the brace I had plundered earlier. The joint turned very lightly and smoothly, and the degree of movement could be precisely calibrated. After I had gathered all materials, I spent a day putting my new invention together. I then fine-tuned it to make sure it worked well. I fixed a piece of elastic between the pull string and the device to make sure Sze Sze could not pull it off the table. I then connected the switch to the computer and tried it out. It worked perfectly—for me.

It is one thing to design, build and test an instrument and make it do what it is supposed to do; it is quite a different story to expect someone who is severely affected by cerebral palsy to operate such a contrivance. After I had booted up the computer and selected the WiVik program, I introduced my latest invention to Sze Sze and demonstrated how it worked. She looked at it with interest, but her face did not betray what she thought of my latest brainchild. She probably had seen enough of my inventions, contraptions that didn't live up to expectation. I attached the pull string to her left arm, the arm over which she has the best control, and asked her to write *the*. When the cursor highlighted the letter *t*, she had no problem pulling the string, but she couldn't return her arm to the rest position; she also got her fingers entangled in the pull string. After a few more futile attempts, I tried having her operate the device with her foot. That didn't go any better.

Auntie Wendy had been following the whole procedure with great interest. She suggested, "Perhaps Sze Sze can use her head to operate the contraption." That seemed like a sensible suggestion. Although Sze Sze's neck muscles are too weak to support the weight of her head, within the confines of her neck brace, she has fairly good control over the movements of her head. "Let's see," Wendy mused, "I think I have just the right thing for her."

Wendy left to search her store of splints, restraints and other devices she had made over the years for different members of the family. Soon she returned with something that resembled a soft helmet with a pointer, which could be fitted over Sze Sze's head. We attached the string to the end of the pointer and adjusted the length of it. When Sze Sze looked at the screen, the switch was in the off position. Then, when the cursor reached the desired letter, she turned her head away from the screen. When she looked back at the screen, she could see the result of her action and bring the switch back to its off position at the same time. The result was somewhat better than having her operate the switch with either arm or leg, but not by much. The problem was that her neck muscles tire easily, and even within the confined space of her neck brace, there was too much play to have consistent results. It proved to be another exercise in futility.

Not everything we did was fraught with frustration. There were many activities that brought diversion and enjoyment to both Sze Sze and me. One of those was helping Co Co improve her English. This attractive young woman, who was only one month younger than Sze Sze, was a new volunteer to the home. In the evening she attended English classes, and during the day she did her homework and self-study. Every Saturday morning she traveled from her home in the Sham Shui Po area to the Home of Loving Faithfulness to work there. In the afternoon I sat down with her for an hour to answer questions she had saved up during a week of doing her reading assignments.

One Saturday afternoon, after I had given rides to Shaan, Dibs, Fa Fa and Sze Sze, I told the latter, "I'm sorry, dear friend; you will have to entertain yourself for an hour. I promised Co Co to help her with English. I don't think you'll be interested in that." The expression on her face told me I was quite mistaken in that assumption. When I asked her if she wanted to sit in on the lesson, her face lit up. From that day on, I had two English students on Saturday afternoons, one asking all the questions and taking copious notes, the other, auditing the lesson, soaking it all up like a sponge. During one of those sessions Co Co said, "Uncle Bill, this week I was reading Elie Wiesel's *Night*. I found two words that confuse me, the one was *mental* and the other *spiritual*. What exactly is the difference—aren't those words about the same in meaning?"

"No, not really—you see, Co Co, you have a body, a mind and a soul or spirit. Your mind and your spirit are not the same thing. With your mind you think. For anything that has to do with the mind, you can use the adjective *mental*—for example, someone whose mind is sick is said to have a *mental* illness. Now, the word spirit, like mind, is a noun. Our spirit or soul is the principle of our conscious life; it is where our emotions and motivations dwell. It's who you really are. For anything that has to do with your spirit, we use the adjective *spiritual*."

"Uh . . . I think I know what you mean, Uncle Bill, but can you give me an example to show me the real difference between mental and spiritual?"

"Now, let's see, Co Co, if I can make it crystal clear. What we are doing here—for me to explain the difference between the meaning of two words and for you to wrap your mind around it—is a *mental* exercise. I'm racking my brain to explain it to you, and you are stretching your mind to understand it, isn't it?"

"Yes, I now understand that part."

As I cast about for an example to make clear the meaning of the adjective *spiritual*, my eye fell on Sze Sze. She had been following our discussion with the greatest interest. I turned to her and asked, "Sze Sze, do you mind if I use the story of your recent illness to explain to Co Co what *spiritual* means?"

Sze Sze's face broke open in a smile, and her tongue came out.

I turned to Co Co and asked, "Do you know what a Christian is?"

"Yes, it is someone who prays to the God."

"Sze Sze is a Christian. She believes in God—by the way, you don't need to use the article *the* before the word God—she loves God and, yes, she prays to him. Last November—that was before you started volunteering here—she became seriously ill. Between Christmas and New Year, we all thought she would die. During the three months she was in hospital, she underwent three critical operations. She suffered a great deal of pain. It was Sze Sze's desire to die. She wanted to be taken out of this body of pain; she longed to

Sze Sze, My Daughter

go to heaven and be with Jesus. But here she is—still with us. God still has a task for her here on earth. In a way, she was disappointed that God did not take her home; on the other hand, she is happy to be alive, to have found a new friend in you, Co Co. We have been praying for someone her own age to befriend her."

I looked at those two young women, one beautiful, healthy and vibrant, the other recovering from serious illness, wheelchair bound and completely dependent on others. Co Co was holding Sze Sze's hand; they were smiling at each other. I continued, "Before she became ill, Sze Sze loved Jesus. She knew He would never leave her, that He would always be with her and help her in times of trouble. But when she was lying there in that hospital bed, crying out in pain, she experienced that Jesus was actually there with her. He helped her cope with pain and, yes, with the disappointment of not being taken to heaven at that time. This experience has given her a deeper love for God."

All the time I was telling Sze Sze's story, I was watching closely her reaction. I didn't want to say anything she would not want me to tell. I need not have worried. Her eyes were shiny, and her tongue kept sliding out in agreement to what I was saying. I went on, "What happened to Sze Sze's body was a physical experience. What happened to her as a person was more than something that touched her mind—it was an experience that touched her spirit, it strengthened her character, it deepened her faith in God, it changed her as a person—in short, it was her *spiritual* journey."

When I finished my explanation, Co Co had tears in her eyes. She said, "Now I understand, Uncle Bill." She then turned to Sze Sze and asked, "Do you really love God; did He really help you when you were sick?"

Sze Sze's smile answered Co Co's question.

"Uncle Bill, how can Sze Sze be so strong? How did she learn about God?"

"Sze Sze first learned about Jesus in school. Her physiotherapist, a Christian lady, taught her about the love of Jesus. Sze Sze also is part of a Christian family, where she learns more about God. I have also written devotions, short lessons, about parts of the Bible, and we study them together. It is the Holy Spirit who works faith in Sze Sze's heart, so that she believes what she has been taught about God."

"Oh—may I read those lessons, Uncle Bill? I want to know how they have helped Sze Sze."

Sze Sze, My Daughter

"You will have to ask Sze Sze if she wants to share them with you, Co Co."

She turned to Sze Sze, who was beaming. She readily consented to give her new friend a copy of the devotions on Psalm 23.

After Co Co had left for home, Sze Sze and I talked about the things we had discussed with her. "You know, Sze Sze," I said, "I may have done all the talking, but I was only your mouth piece. What I told Co Co was really your testimony, the story of what God has done in your life. Who knows—God may use it to bring your new friend to a true saving faith in him. Perhaps, you telling your story to others may be the purpose God has for your life." It was a very happy young woman I wheeled into her bedroom at the end of the day. At devotion time we prayed for Co Co, and we thanked God that he had answered our prayer for sending a new friend into Sze Sze's life, one who was about the same age as she was.

Fu Fu came to the home soon after it opened its doors in 1965. He is unable to speak or do anything at all. He sits quietly in his wheelchair, looking at nothing in particular and waving his arms as if directing an orchestra. When he is content, he makes happy grunts. There are times when he, for some unexplainable reason, bursts out into laughter, merriment so infectious that those around him can't help but join in. One day, while I was giving Sze Sze her evening meal, Fu Fu had one of his laughing spells. Sze Sze also began to laugh and promptly choked on the mouthful of food I had just given her. After she had calmed down and I had cleaned up her tray, I wondered out loud what it was that made Fu Fu so happy.

As I continued to feed Sze Sze, I had to think of the difference between Fu Fu and her. One is living in his own private world, apparently oblivious to what is happening around him, yet, has moments of joy in his life that causes him to burst out laughing. The other is fully alive and painfully aware of the world in which she lives but unable to participate in its affairs. I looked at her. She seemed engrossed in her own thoughts. "Sze Sze," I said, "I have a question I probably have no right to ask—remember," I reminded her, "you don't have to answer if you don't want to." I looked at her eyes. They told me it was okay to go on. "Well, here it is: If you had a choice, would you choose to stay as you are now, or would you rather be like Fu Fu? Do you want to answer this question?"

Sze Sze looked at me, thought a while and showed me her tongue.

"Well, would you want to stay as you are now?" I looked at her for her reaction. There was none. I waited a little longer; then I asked, "Would you rather be like Fu Fu?" She waited a long moment. I could almost see her mind turning over the question, looking at it from every side, and she slowly brought out her tongue. "Is it because he doesn't realize what life could be like for him . . . because he doesn't know what he is missing?" As she answered affirmatively, her eyes began to fill with tears.

"I'm sorry," I whispered, "I shouldn't make you sad by asking such crazy questions." Her reaction surprised me. She looked at me in that special way, that says, "Why not?"

"Is it because you completely trust me as your friend that you dare to make yourself vulnerable?"

Yes.

"Then I dare to ask another question; it has been on my mind for some time. I read in your file that you are considered to be severely mentally handicapped. Now, we both know that this assessment is completely wrong. However, do you think that you are somewhat mentally retarded?"

She looked at me thoughtfully and answered yes.

"Well, dear friend, I have good news for you. I disagree with you. Just because people sometimes treat you as someone who is mentally disabled does not mean that you are. I know that people sometimes talk *about* you rather than *to* you. They think you will not understand what they are saying. They sometimes make decisions *for* you without consulting *with* you. Often they are decisions you could and should make for yourself. They also use simple, childish language hoping you will understand them. But you know what? They are mistaken when they think there is something mentally wrong with you—and so are you!"

Sze Sze stared at me, not knowing what to think or believe.

I continued, "You know what kind of work I used to do in Canada, don't you. I've taught for many years students who had trouble learning. Some had problems because they were somewhat mentally retarded, others because they had learning disabilities of one kind or another. Now, those two things are not the same. I know some very intelligent people who have a learning disability. I have worked with you long enough to know whether or not you are mentally handicapped. Will you believe me when I tell you that you are not?"

I waited. "I don't see your tongue, Sze Sze" I said. "Does this mean you don't believe me . . . you don't know what to believe . . .

have you believed so long you are retarded, that what I tell you comes as a shock—a pleasant shock to you?"

As she slowly brought out her tongue, tears began to course down her cheeks.

I moved aside her bowl of food, took both her hands in mine and waited before I went on, "You know, my dear friend, I suspect, but I'm not yet absolutely sure, that you may have a learning disability—that will keep you from learning how to spell. You came to this home at the age of nine. You were labeled as severely physically and mentally disabled, and you had been treated that way. There is no doubt about your physical condition, but that doctors and psychologists, social workers and other professionals who worked with classified you as severely mentally handicapped was not just a big mistake. It was a crime."

I paused to let Sze Sze think about what I had told her. Then I went on, "Fortunately, the Aunties knew better than all the experts who had stuck the wrong label on you. They soon decided that you were much smarter than the reports said. They looked for ways to develop your abilities. They first sent you to Hong Chi Pine Hill Village School and then to Elaine Fields School. You must have been almost ten when you were became a student there . . . . What a terrible waste of time!"

I tried to imagine how much more Sze Sze could have learned had she been properly assessed and gone there as kindergarten student rather than a ten-year-old trying to play catch-up. She definitely is not mentally handicapped, but because of the postponement of her education, she was developmentally delayed. I know she had learned much at Elaine Fields, but the best years for learning important skills had been lost. It was impossible to catch up on everything she had missed out on by starting her real education so late, and what we were trying to do now would undo only part of the damage caused by that delay.

I looked at Sze Sze's bowl; it was still half full, "I've been talking too much. Everyone has finished and you are only halfway done. You want to finish this? It's quite cold by now." It took more than digesting my long, rambling speech to kill Sze Sze's appetite. I finished feeding her, brought her to her bedroom where the caregivers were waiting for her and said, "See you at devotion time."

Sze Sze shares a large bedroom with mainly male members of the family. One of them, Tak Tak, an epileptic boy in his mid-teens, lives in his own private world. His focus is on anything he can put into his mouth, food or fiber. He will deftly pick at the fabric of his clothes, especially the left sleeve of whatever he is wearing, until he is able to pull out some fibers and eat them. From there on it will be systematically demolished and ingested. He may leave in the morning with a new shirt on his back, but by the time he returns in the afternoon, there will be little left of his sleeve.

Caregivers at the home are instructed to protect the privacy of the family. Staff at the home, which, except for the office manager and the two chauffeurs, is made up entirely of women, interprets this as protecting the dignity of the female members of the family. More than once have I seen them walk Tak Tak to the bathing area, completely naked and in full view of the other members of the family. For most of them, male or female, it makes little or no difference whether or not they or others are exposed, because they are either blind or unaware of physical differences between male and female.

One morning I was visiting Sze Sze in her bedroom; she was not feeling well and had been ordered bed rest. I was seated beside her bed and talking, watching her face, as I usually do, for her reactions. Suddenly, I lost her attention. Her eyes shot past me to Tak Tak's cage-bed in the corner of the room. One of the caregivers had completely stripped him of his night clothes, helped him out of his cage and led him to the bathing area. Sze Sze followed him with her eyes as far as she could.

After Tak Tak had left the bedroom, I looked at Sze Sze and asked, "Is this the first time you have seen him like this . . . undressed?"

No.

"Have you often seen him naked?"

Yes.

"Would you like Tak Tak or me watch you if you were completely undressed?"

No.

"Yet, you like to watch him like this?"

Yes.

"Do you think that is right?"

No.

Looking straight at me, without blushing or blinking, Sze Sze answered my questions. I admired her complete honesty. She trusted I would understand. I did. Here was a young woman, twenty years old, physically disabled but probably with a healthy sex drive and a natural curiosity about the opposite sex. She knew that, because of her condition, her physical desires would never be met or fulfilled.

I was upset and angry about the duplicity of it all. On the one hand, staff was almost paranoid about safeguarding the privacy of the women and girls in the family; on the other hand, they didn't give a tinker's damn that they violated the dignity of the men and boys. But there was another issue here. I wondered how this kind of exposure affected Sze Sze's emotional, psychological and spiritual wellbeing. What kind of guidance had this young woman received in the early stages of sexual awakening to help her cope with physical changes, urges and desires. What kind of counseling did she now receive to help her accept and deal with a life of abstinence. Surely, regular exposure to young men parading before her in the buff could not have been helpful to her in dealing with those questions. It would only arouse unhealthy sexual desires and lead to sinful longings and daydreams. When I brought up this issue with Wendy, she referred me to Pui Yee, who was in charge of staff issues; when I approached Pui Yee, she told me staff had been instructed to treat all members of the family in the same way. And that was the end of it.

"Please, stay a moment, there is something I must tell you before you go home." It was the end of the morning chapel service on the last day of our stay in Hong Kong. Wendy and Pui Yee had already left chapel; they had seemed upset about something. Valerie stood at the door, her hand on its knob. As she walked back to her seat, Ena and I followed and also sat down again. She began to speak and then broke down. When she could continue, she said, "Sandy has been arrested." We looked at her, not knowing what to make of that statement.

Sandy was one of the hundreds of thousands of destitute Filipino domestic workers, who flock to Hong Kong and other parts of the world to find employment. She had been hired seven or eight months earlier to help Aunties Joan and Irena with household chores. These elderly ladies, friends of the home, occupied the apartments in the older part of the home. Other Filipinos working at the home wondered if there was a curse on Sandy's family. Over a period of five years, her family had suffered an unusual number of tragedies. Her husband had been killed in an industrial accident; her father had died under suspicious circumstances; her only child, a daughter, had been kidnapped, raped and murdered. After each tragedy, she had appealed to her church community—the same church Wendy attended—for financial help to pay for her airfare to the Philippines and cover the cost of funerals.

Sandy had also been the first victim of the thefts that had occurred at the home in the past year. She claimed someone had made off with her purse, which held her passport and Hong Kong ID. She had gone through much trouble getting those documents replaced. Recently, she had been allowed a few days off to attend a church camp for young adults. A few days later, her pastor received a telephone call from Sandy's sister, a domestic helper in Singapore, who was worried about her sister. She had found a text message on her phone in which Sandy asked her to take care of her daughter in case something happened to her. The pastor was puzzled. He remembered that Sandy's only daughter had died under tragic circumstances. He became suspicious and called the police, who had Sandy arrested. Over a period of five years, Sandy had defrauded her church community of more than one hundred thousand dollars.

Preliminary investigations uncovered that Sandy's father, husband and daughter were alive and well in the Philippines. It also revealed she had never attended the church camp for young adults. Instead, she had visited her sister in Singapore. When the police searched her room, they found not only her new passport and Hong Kong ID but also those she claimed had been stolen.

As Valerie told us all this, I wondered if Sandy was responsible for the things that had gone missing in the home, including Sze Sze's computer. It obviously had been an inside job. Whoever had helped herself to the purses, pocketbooks and computer knew exactly when the intended victims were not in their rooms or offices. It wasn't that the people she had robbed were faceless victims. She knew all of them intimately, the Aunties, Anna and Sze Sze. She had often chatted amiably with Sze Sze.

Needless to say, Ena and I were shocked. I wondered how anyone could stoop so low as to rob a severely handicapped person of her computer, a tool she needed to learn how to communicate better. And so another busy and emotion-packed visit came to an end.

Chapter 12

We returned to Hong Kong in October 2005. It was good to see how well Sze Sze had recovered; she looked healthy and had put on weight. Our young friend looked fully alive, was brimming with mischief and greeted me with an adoring smile. Once Ena and I had adjusted to the difference in time, we got into our regular routine. Mealtimes were good for talking. One day as I was feeding Sze Sze, I commented on how well she looked. "Remember how sick you were almost one year ago?"

She looked serious as she answered my question.

"People all over the world were praying for your recovery. Isn't it wonderful how the Lord has answered those prayers?" In response, Sze Sze screwed up her mouth, a sign of strong emotion. I looked at her and asked, "Do you still feel God has robbed you of heaven?"

She answered with a very definite yes, and tears began to flow. It made me wonder what she had experienced at that time. I ventured a guess. "When you were close to death, did God give you a glimpse of heaven?"

A wistful smile slowly spread over her face. "Is that the reason you long so much for heaven?"

Yes.

"You are indeed a privileged young woman, Sze Sze, but you know what? There must be a reason why the Lord did not call you home to celebrate Christmas with him in heaven last year. He must still have a task for you here on earth. All of us are placed here on earth with a purpose—you know that, don't you?"

She looked at me with her large, black eyes as if to say, What would He expect me to do? I continued, "I have no idea what that task is, Sze Sze, but you have quite a story to tell—remember the last time I was here. You allowed me to share your testimony with Co Co." A smile spread over her face when I mentioned that event. Sze Sze and Co Co had become close friends during our absence. "Perhaps God wants you to share your story with others to bring them to himself. As long as He doesn't call you to heaven, you will still have work to do on earth."

It touches me to see how much this young woman longs for heaven. Part of the reason is, of course, her desire to be set free from the body which has held her spirit hostage for so long, but it is not just that. Although there are times she is confused about what God has in mind for her, and moments she questions his fairness and justice, she does really love him with a deep devotion.

Sze Sze may not be able to express that love in words, but her expressive face sometimes speaks more eloquently than words. She displayed her deep longing to see Jesus quite visibly one day when Mrs. Yoshida came to play for the family. We had gathered in chapel, Junko played the piano and I my mandolin. Those of us who had voices sang all the favorite songs of the family. For Ping Pong it was *Amazing Grace*, for Dibs *Shine, Jesus, Shine*, for Sze Sze *Give Thanks, with a Grateful Heart* and for one of the volunteers *How Great Thou Art*. I watched Sze Sze when we came to the third stanza of that powerful hymn: "When Christ shall come 'mid shouts of acclamation and calls me home, what joy shall fill my heart," her face was radiant and her tongue came out repeatedly to show her agreement with those words. It made me jealous of her. I wished I could look forward to the day of Christ's return with that same longing and intensity she does.

Yet, a few days can make so much difference. Two days after that hymn sing in chapel, Sze Sze was restless at evening devotions. She could not lie still one minute, did not pay any attention to what I said and did a lot of vocalizing. Sometimes she does this to show assent to what I am saying. This time was different. It was almost a show of defiance. I was going to tell her about the importance of showing reverence when we are talking about God and his Word. However, one good look at her told me an admonition at that time would make little impression. Instead I asked, "You are very restless tonight, Sze Sze. Are you upset about something—do you want to talk about it?"

Yes, and she began to cry.

Some probing brought to light her problem. Why would God allow her bright mind to be imprisoned by her uncooperative body? I talked about some of the things I had mentioned before, when she had gone through a period of questioning God's fairness. Then we had a time of prayer. That, of course, did not solve her problem, but I kept hoping and praying that a time may come, when she can accept her condition and have peace with it. After I had prayed with her, she didn't want me to go. I promised that, after I had said goodnight to all the others, I would come back to her. I did. She just wanted me to sit quietly with her and hold her hand. Then, after another short prayer, she let me go.

After I had returned to our room, I wondered what had brought on Sze Sze's bout of sadness and questioning. Usually, it is something that has happened during the day, an incident which has touched her emotionally, something that triggered it. We went through the events of the day. Ena suggested, "Perhaps it was Hannah."

I looked at her and asked, "What about Hannah?" Hannah was a member of Pete and Sue's household. She was a bright and most beautiful two-year-old, the child of a Thai domestic helper and a Chinese father. The mother, who at the time of Hannah's birth was illegally in Hong Kong, had abandoned her child, but she had refused to sign her over to Social Services and had left Hong Kong. This left her daughter in legal limbo: she couldn't be adopted because she had no right of abode. The Home of Loving Faithfulness had been asked to take her in until a way out could be found for her.

That afternoon, while I was teaching Sze Sze, Hannah had wandered into our kitchen and tried to climb up on my knee. I had picked her up, given her a hug and placed her on the tray of Sze Sze's wheelchair. It was a most tender scene. The girls had hugged each other, and Hannah had given Sze Sze a kiss. They just sat there, smiling at each other until Hannah became restless and moved on.

"I wonder...," said Ena, who had witnessed it all. "It is possible Sze Sze is upset because she realizes she will never hold in her arms a little girl of her own. Her condition robs her of all the things we so easily take for granted: dating, courtship, marriage and a family." It seemed like an acceptable explanation of Sze Sze's spell of sadness.

We were not successful in making the computer more accessible for Sze Sze. Our latest attempt—using a head pointer—had proven to be as useless as all the other ways we had tried. Even before I gave it a try, I knew it wouldn't work. In all our other attempts, I had always had a glimmer of hope that we might hit upon something that would work. Using a head pointer was almost like an act of desperation. We had come to the end of our tether. I could think of only one other way that might work for her: eye gaze technology, but it is prohibitively expensive. Since Sze Sze's interest in her studies was beginning to flag, there was no way I could justify persuading the home to invest thirty to forty thousand dollars in an eye gaze computer.

Yes, Sze Sze's interest in her studies had reached low ebb; she was becoming more and more frustrated. So was I. One reason was our failure to find a satisfactory way for Sze Sze to access her computer, the other her by now obvious learning disability which kept her from achieving any measurable success in spelling.

I am not sure what kept me from making the decision to drop the subject—my promise to respect her choices, admission I had failed—whatever it was, in hindsight, it would have been the wiser thing to do. Her frustration even affected her enjoyment of reading. One morning, after we had put Dibs on the Rehabus, I wheeled my student into the classroom and said, "Time to do some reading, Sze Sze, you haven't read for a coon's age." She turned to me a face that was hard to interpret. I chose to ignore it, prepared her tray by mounting the reading board on it and asked her to choose a story. She looked the other way. I said, "Sze Sze, look at me. Are you going to read?"

She again turned her face to me. Her eyes were neither angry nor defiant. They had a look of defeat.

"So, my friend, it looks like you are not going to read today. Do you want a break from your studies."

No reaction but an empty look.

"Are you through with reading?"

Yes.

"For good?"

Yes. She had become frustrated to the point where she wanted to quit everything, spelling, reading and working with her computer.

I looked at her and understood her frustration. I, too, felt disheartened about my inability to find a better way for her to access her computer. I, too, felt disappointed I was unable to find a way around her spelling block. Looking at the row of binders with stories and spelling lessons on the kitchen counter, materials I had developed for her over the past three years, I gestured at them and asked, "Do you want me to get rid of all this?"

She gave them a cursory glance. Yes.

"Well, then you will have to help me bring the lot to my room." I removed the reading board from Sze Sze's tray and piled on the binders. I pushed her chair out of the kitchen, through the living room and into the sunshine. We made our way past the Play Room and the staff dining room and through the narrow passage between the kitchen and offices to the elevator. I wheeled her chair into the lift

Sze Sze, My Daughter

and pushed the button. We came to our room—we lived once again on the second floor of the B Block, this time in a room vacated by Auntie Val. Ena looked surprised and exclaimed, "Visitors so early in the morning!—My, you don't look very happy, Sze Sze. Come to think of it, neither do you, Bill. Had a fight, you two?"

Sze Sze began to cry. While I removed the binders from her tray and put them on a shelf in one of the closets, I explained to Ena that we were taking a break from our studies. I then wiped away Sze Sze's tears while I tried to hold back my own, sat across from her and asked, "Do you think we should have a good talk together—you, Sze Sze, Ena and I?" She thought this a good idea.

"We should first tell you what this is all about," I said as I turned to Ena. "Sze Sze has been working hard to learn how to read, spell and use the computer. She has done very well in reading, but spelling has been harder than she and I thought it would be. Accessing her computer, as you know, has also been a struggle. Because of this, she has become frustrated. So have I. Now Sze Sze has decided to throw in the towel. She has decided to stop all her lessons. She even wants to stop reading altogether—right, Sze Sze?"

While I was talking, she had placed her hand on mine as if to comfort me. Yes.

"Now, what do you think of all this, Ena?"

Ena looked at Sze Sze and asked, "How old are you? About to turn twenty-one, I believe. How many more years do you think you will live . . . five . . . fifteen . . . twenty-five? We don't really know when the Lord will call you home, do we. However few or many it may be, try to picture what those years will be like. There you will be, sitting in your chair, waiting for someone to take time to talk to you or put you in front of a television set. You hope, of course, it will be a show you like, because, if it isn't, you cannot turn it off or change the channel. You have learned how to read—perhaps you can learn how to handle an e-book reader. Now, if we can also find a way in which you can access your computer—don't give up hope yet—you will be able to do so many other things." She paused; then she went on, "I hope you will think carefully before you make a decision. Think of all the time and effort you have put into learning to read and spell and use the computer. Then think about what life will be like if you decide to throw it all away."

"I think this is good advice, don't you think so, Sze Sze," I said. "Let's think and pray about it. The decision you will make today may

Sze Sze, My Daughter

affect you the rest of your life. How much time do you think you will need—let's see, today is Thursday—will you know by Sunday?"

No.

"How about five days . . . one week?"

Yes.

We had a time of prayer together. I then brought Sze Sze to the Play Room and returned to our apartment. I felt for my young friend. She had tried so hard, but she had so many strikes against her. She had bravely wrestled with her handicaps and shown much resilience, but now she had reached a dead end, a point where she could no longer bring up the energy needed to rally her fighting spirit. I asked myself if I had pushed her too hard or too far. Often, when the going got tough, I had asked her if she wanted to stop, but her proud spirit did not allow for defeat. She had always wanted to push on, to forge ahead. Perhaps I should have decided for her and dropped spelling from our program. I recalled my plans to break open the bars of her prison. I thought of the time and energy I had expended on teaching her—Sze Sze was the main reason I had returned time and again to Hong Kong. I felt deflated.

After tea I took Sze Sze for a short walk to the garden and sat on the edge of the barbeque pit. She looked at her communication board, and her hand began to move across it.

"What is it you are telling me, my friend?" I watched as her hand slowly moved from *l* to *o* and then stopped moving.

She looked at me as if to say: You can guess the rest.

"I know a lot of words beginning with those two letters, Sze Sze, but I need more clues. Her hand moved to *s*.

"*L . . . o . . . s . . . .* Oh, you have lost something," I said, knowing this was not true.

No. Her tears began to flow.

"Sze Sze, you are not spelling the word *loser,* are you?"

Slowly her tongue came out.

"And who are you calling loser . . . *me* . . . *yourself?*"

She was.

"You know, my dear friend, perhaps I am the loser. I had so many plans for you, and I have failed in most of them. True, you have done well in reading, and I'm sure you will do even better if you decide to keep up with your reading lessons. But I failed in teaching you how to write, and making it possible for you to access your computer hasn't been a great success, has it. So, you could say, if there is a loser here, it is Bill. I have raised your hopes and let you down . . . I have failed you as teacher, don't you agree?"

There was no response, so I continued, "I'm sure you can tell I'm frustrated—no, you're not the only one—but you know what, Sze Sze, I refuse to admit I'm a loser. I will never be able to feel the frustration you experience every day, but don't *you* dare call yourself a loser. Even if you decide not to continue with any of your lessons, there will be no losers—only winners! Look at what we have gained these four years: We've become the best of friends, and we've gained each other's respect. I have taught you how to read, and you have taught me patience and sensitivity to those who live with disabilities—and in the process, we've had a lot of fun. These have been wonderful years, and no one can rob us of what we have experienced together. *Losers?* No, we're both winners!" I dried her tears and said, "Belen will wonder what has happened to you. I better rush you back to your bedroom before we both get into trouble." I brought her to the bedroom and said, "See you in an hour at devotions."

Sze Sze didn't need a week to make her decision. On Sunday afternoon she was sitting in front of the television in the Play Room. I don't know if she had been watching whatever program was on, but the moment I entered the room, she turned to me and became very excited. I took her to the garden and asked, "You've made a decision, haven't you—want to tell me about it?" She did. She flung up her arms, threw back her head and laughed loudly.

"Let me guess," I said, "you've decided to continue with your lessons. Wonderful! Now, listen my friend, I've also done some thinking; I, too, have made a decision. If it is alright with you, we will continue with reading, but, perhaps, we should forget about spelling. We communicate very well without you spelling things out for me. I don't think it's worth all the frustration to teach you a skill you will likely use little to communicate your thoughts. What do you think?" Sze Sze agreed and promptly turned her head, directing me with her eyes to where our apartment was. "You see what I mean, my friend," I said, and I sang: *"Your eyes will tell me all I want to know,"*[15] a line from one of her favorite songs. "I can read you like an open book, my girl. Your eyes are telling me, that you want to share your decision with Ena, right!—Who needs spelling!—She will be happy to hear about it."

We've celebrated Sze Sze's twenty-first birthday. Ena and I treated her to a dinner on the eve of her birthday. We told her she could ask a friend to come with her, and she chose Dibs. There was a time she barely tolerated Dibs because of her bouts of jealousy. All this changed after Dibs joined Sze Sze at Wah Sum Centre. It is good she has a friend again at the home. Her last friend, Yin Fan, died two years ago.

Kim, who is allowed to drive again, drove us to *The Better 'Ole* in Fanling. Staff at the restaurant was very helpful in rearranging tables to accommodate two wheelchairs. Sze Sze, who relishes good food, chose spaghetti bolognaise from the set menu, which included a bowl of borscht and half a dozen escargots, and whatever Sze Sze chose, Dibs also wanted. While we waited for our dishes to be served, we helped Sze Sze open her birthday card. It held our present to her, a pair of tickets to the newly opened Hong Kong Disneyland. The girls were over the moon. Their exclamations of joy attracted the attention and smiles of other guests at the restaurant. The amusement park is completely wheelchair friendly; people in wheelchairs and those who accompany them need not cue up, they can move right up to the head of the line.

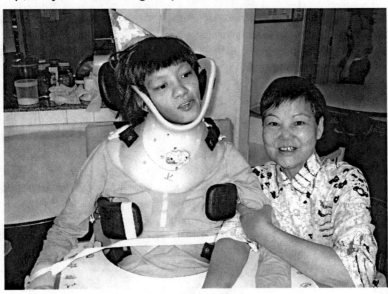

Sze Sze and her mother

On Sze Sze's birthday, her mother was the first to arrive with a large birthday cake for her daughter—the first of four she would receive that day. She also brought Styrofoam containers with wonton, almond cakes and other Chinese delicacies for Ena and me, her way of showing appreciation for our involvement in her daughter's life.

Sze Sze, My Daughter

After greeting Sze Sze, she attached herself to us and, as she usually does when she visits, directed at us an endless stream of chatter. Even repeated reminders that we can't understand Cantonese didn't stop the flow of whatever it was she wanted to tell us.

She then turned to Sze Sze. Again, there was that unbroken stream of verbosity, this time uttered in a whiny tone of voice and directed at her daughter. Sze Sze tolerated her for some time until she'd had enough. She then turned to her mother with an angry snarl. We had witnessed scenes like that before.

Sze Sze claims she loves her mother, and I believe her, but it doesn't always show. She always is happy when her mother makes an appearance, usually once a month. But observing the conversation between mother and daughter—a misnomer, perhaps—I have noticed, that the mother has never learned to communicate with her daughter. She will never ask Sze Sze questions and wait for her to answer. She literally unloads on her daughter. Those who can understand her tell us that she dumps on Sze Sze all her problems. She will complain about her husband, who left her for another woman; about her health problems, which are considerable; about having lost a teenaged son; about Auntie Wendy, who was willing to adopt two children with disabilities but unwilling to adopt her daughter; and about having a disabled and retarded daughter. Yes, she regards Sze Sze as mentally retarded. She discharges all her unhappiness and discontent on her daughter. She fails to realize this poor girl has enough problems of her own—including a mother who doesn't understand her. Sze Sze has become tired of listening repeatedly to the same litany of her mother's complaints.

In a way I can understand Sze Sze's reaction; on the other hand there is something not right about it. The day after her birthday we read a devotion based on Romans 2:6. It states God "will render to every man according to his works." I asked Sze Sze if she fully understood what those words mean. She wasn't sure. I began, "You know, of course, that we are not saved because of all the good things we do in life—we are saved by grace—but once we have been saved, we are expected to live lives that are different, lives that reflect the love of God. It should show in the way we treat others. You understand that, don't you?"

Yes.

"In heaven we will receive special rewards for the good deeds we have done on earth. That includes how we treat people we meet in daily life . . . people like your mother." I looked at Sze Sze and said, "Your mother and brother may well be watching you. They may wonder if being a Christian will make any difference in your behavior. It is good that you pray regularly for their conversion, but treating your mother with disrespect may well keep them from becoming Christians. Do I make sense?

"Try to understand your mother, Sze Sze," I continued. "She's had a difficult life. Her youngest son died in his teens and you, her only daughter, are disabled. Your father, instead of being a support to her, has unjustly blamed your mother for your condition and used that as an excuse for leaving her, forcing her to bring up three children by herself. That must have been very hard on her. Your mother is in poor health—you know that. For the past dozen or so years she has been battling cancer. I don't need to tell you that her life has been far from happy.

"Sometimes you go through hard times, Sze Sze, and, like your mother, focus too much on your problems—but there's a difference. You have Someone who helps you through your rough spots; you have a Good Shepherd who helps carry your burden. He has promised never to leave or forsake you. But your mother—who or what does she have, does she know the Lord? No. All she can do is focus on her problems. She has no one who will help her carry her load. So, when she comes to visit you, she unloads on you—I know it isn't fair that she does—and you are unable to help her. You can't even tell her who helps you carry your burden when it becomes too heavy for you to bear. So you snarl at her in frustration. Listen, dear friend, I'm not condemning you. I just want to make you see that this kind of behavior helps neither you nor your mother. You understand this, don't you?"

She did, and she began to cry.

I put my arm around her and said, "It's not always easy to be a Christian, is it? I hope you don't get the feeling I'm telling you how to live, or that I'm trying to change your character. I can't. But as a fellow Christian, it is my duty to point out things I see in your life that are a poor witness. I hope that, when you see things in my life that are a poor testimony, you will let me know there's something wrong in my behavior—I know you will; you have done it in the past." I dried her tears and we had a time of prayer. When I wished her a good night, she gave me a kiss, something she hadn't done since we had returned to Hong Kong more than a month ago.

One evening after finishing devotions, I asked Sze Sze to pray for me. I hadn't felt well for a number of days and wanted to take a break from my activities. When I asked her the following evening if she had prayed for me, she answered that she hadn't. I told her, "I admire your honesty, but I'm a puzzled and disappointed. In the past when I've asked you to remember me in your prayers, you've always done so." As I went from bed to bed, I kept thinking about her and wondered if there was something bothering her. She had seemed different these last few days, less exuberant and more pensive—almost brooding. After I had made the last stop in my rounds, I went back to her. She hadn't turned to the wall as she normally does when going to sleep. Her troubled eyes were focused on the ceiling above her. She looked surprised when she saw me. I asked, "Are you having a hard time? Do you find it hard to pray—not just for me—but for anything at all, for yourself?"

Yes. A look of relief spread over her face. Bill understood.

"Is that why you haven't prayed for me?"

Yes.

"I'm sorry, Sze Sze, forgive me for being so dull, for making you feel guilty. If you want to, we will talk more about your problems tomorrow."

She smiled, turned to the wall and closed her eyes.

It is disconcerting how Sze Sze's condition affects not only the physical aspects of her life but also its social, emotional, and spiritual dimensions. Not only must others do for her the things they so habitually do for themselves; when they see changes in her behavior, they also need to take time to ask the right questions. Knowing that in the past she had always faithfully prayed for me when I had asked her, I should immediately have realized there was a reason why this time she hadn't. Before telling her I was puzzled and disappointed, making her feel guilty, I should have probed deeper to find out what was troubling her. Not doing so could have affected our relationship, upset her emotionally and harmed her spiritually. I was grateful I had gone back to her and asked what troubled her.

The following morning, Sze Sze looked far from happy, so I asked her if she wanted to talk about what was troubling her. She wanted me to take her to chapel, the place where we usually carried on our serious discussions. "Are you in pain?" There was no response. "Is it a pain deep inside?" This time she answered yes.

I knew what the problem was, and I decided to meet it head on. "You are lonely because you have no one to call your own, aren't you?" She acknowledged my guess was correct and began to weep. "You are in love with a married man who is old enough to be your grandfather."

Yes. I knew it. Lately her looks had betrayed her.

It wrenched my heart to look at this picture of sadness and hopelessness. I replied, "You realize, of course, that I cannot respond to this kind of love in the same way. Ena is number one in my life. I can love you as a friend—my best friend. Even better, I can love you as my daughter. I would be proud to call you my daughter, but nothing more. You understand that, don't you?"

She understood.

How could this have happened again? I do confess I am fond of her—perhaps too fond? I often let her know how much I appreciate her as a friend. I tried to examine my heart but realized it "is deceitful above all things" and hard to plumb its depths. It is so easy to fool oneself. Had I been giving her mixed signals? Were there in the recesses of my heart emotions of which I wasn't aware but which she felt. I was confused. I'm probably the only man who ever pays attention to her, who treats her as a normal person. We do spend much time together: I feed her and teach her, I do devotions with her in the evening, but I try to be as transparent as possible. When I teach her, the door to the room is always wide open; when I do devotions, there are always others present, Ena or one of the staff.

"Tell me, Sze Sze, am I a temptation to you?"

Yes.

For a moment I struggled. Then I decided it prudent—or was it delusive?—not to tell her that, at times, she also poses a temptation for me. Despite her disabilities, Sze Sze is a young woman of considerable charm. "If I would stop coming to Hong Kong, would that help you?"

No.

Out of sight would not mean out of heart or mind to her. Strong emotions like hers could not be turned on or off like a faucet; they needed to be carefully guided into acceptable channels. But how?

"You know, dear friend, we both need to pray that God will keep our friendship pure."

In the afternoon, while Sze Sze had her nap, I discussed the problem with Ena. She is such a wonderful wife; she completely trusts me. We considered not returning to Hong Kong if that would help our young friend, and we decided to monitor the situation between now and our return to Canada.

At devotion time, I told Sze Sze that I had discussed our problem with Ena. We then talked some more about our situation and what to do about it. We promised to pray regularly for each other.

I told her I needed prayer as much as she did. When Ena came to say goodnight to Sze Sze, she said, "I understand you love Bill. So do I—but I just happened to come first in his life. But you know what? I still love you, and I promise to pray for both of you." She then kissed Sze Sze goodnight.

The next day Ena and I left for Changsha, the capital of Hunan Province, to visit Yin Yi Bing, a former student from our China days. It would be good for Sze Sze and me to put some distance between ourselves.

When we returned one week later, one look at Sze Sze's face told me our problem was still there. I didn't know how to get through to her. How could I make plain to her that this was more than an emotional or social problem, that, at heart, it was a spiritual question. One evening I asked her, "Do you remember you told me that, when you were close to death, you had a glimpse of heaven? Are you looking forward to see that foretaste of heaven become real?"

A slow smile spread over her face, and her tongue showed. "Do you realize you could miss out on heaven?"

She shot me a questioning look. "I am sure you know what adultery is, don't you?" I continued. "Didn't Jesus teach us that any sin, including adultery, is born in our hearts, that thinking about it is as sinful as actually doing it?"

She showed me a reluctant tongue. "Do you think you should change your love for me?"

There was no reaction. I felt I should drive the point home with more force. Although it hurt me, I said, "Listen, Sze Sze, do you think wishing for something—something that will never happen—is worth losing heaven for? The Bible tells us that adulterers, unless they repent of their sins, cannot enter heaven. Unless you repent, dear friend, you will lose out on going to heaven. Do you think it's worth it?"

She cried when she admitted that it would be foolish to forfeit heaven for something that would never become a reality. After we prayed for each other, I wished her a good night.

A few days later, when we made the rounds of the bedrooms, Sze Sze was waiting for me with a contented smile on her face. I pulled up a stool, sat down beside her and asked, "Well, Sze Sze, do you still love this old man?" Her smile told me she did. "Like a friend . . . and nothing more than a friend?"

She smiled and brought out her tongue as far as she could.

"You look happy and content, peaceful," I said. "I have been praying for a long time you would find that kind of peace. In the last devotion on Psalm 23, the sheep says: 'I want to stay with this Shepherd. I don't want to change. I don't want anything in my life to change.' That's quite a statement, isn't it? Can you fully agree with those words, Sze Sze?" I asked. "Are you content with your life as it is . . . including your disability?"

There was a pause. I studied Sze Sze's face. It was serious, but it radiated peace when she answered affirmatively. As I continued to talk with her, she agreed with me that if she had not become disabled, she would not have met Jacqueline who first told her about Jesus and many others, who had helped her in her Christian walk.

A week before Christmas Kim drove us to Disneyland. The day was wonderfully warm, and both Sze Sze and Dibs enjoyed having themselves photographed with Mickey, Goofy and other Disney characters. They were enthralled with the wheelchair accessible rides and the *Golden Mickey Show*. However, *Simba the Lion King Show* proved to be too much for Sze Sze. Wheelchair-bound people were seated in the first row of the theater-in-the-round; they were almost part of the spectacle. The show was very colorful and noisy, and the unexpected, clashing sounds and lightning-like flashes of brightly colored lights startled and panicked her. She grabbed my hand and struggled against the restraints securing her in her chair. Within minutes I had to take her out. We emerged into the bright sunshine, and I looked for a shady spot where I could tidy up her up. I took tissues and cleaned her face, straightened her clothes which had become awry in her struggles, and discovered that one of the Velcro restraints had moved her right pant leg up and scraped the skin off her shin. At a nearby first aid post, they cleaned and dressed her injury. By that time the Simba show had ended, and we walked to the exit of the theater to meet Dibs and Ena.

In the following days, the innocent looking abrasion became infected. Pui Yee took it all quite seriously. She took charge of the healing regimen and decided to experiment with traditional Chinese medication to fight the infection. That treatment included a diet of rice cooked in a large quantity of water. For drinks she was given rice water instead of the coffee she so much enjoys. She was confined to her bedroom as if the wound were highly contagious. Her bed was placed in such a way that the sun would shine on the undressed wound. To accomplish this, her leg was tied to one of the bedrails to keep it in place, and the bed was moved constantly to follow the path of the sun.

Sze Sze, My Daughter

It was a boring time for our young friend. She missed out on the excitement of preparing for the Christmas celebrations, decorating the rooms and trimming the Christmas tree. I spent much time with her in the bedroom, reading to her, doing cross stitch embroidery or just talking. On Christmas morning, while Ena was feeding Sze Sze her watery rice porridge, Pui Yee came breezing into the bedroom, checked Sze Sze's leg and declared she better stay in bed for the rest of the day, and rushed out again, leaving Sze Sze in tears and Ena greatly upset.

Ena told me what had happened. I was livid. I waited until my anger had abated; then I went to the office to speak with Wendy to report on what had happened. "I hope you will not think I'm trying to blackmail you, Wendy," I said, "but if Sze Sze will not be able to attend the Christmas party, there will not be a visit to the home by a genuine, Canadian Father Christmas. I could never enjoy myself playing Santa, knowing Sze Sze would be confined to her bedroom."

"I fully understand," replied Wendy, "I know how close you two are. If you would play Father Christmas while Sze Sze was stuck in her bedroom, it would be a betrayal of your friendship. But don't you worry, as long as I'm in charge here, neither Sze Sze, nor anyone else, will be excluded from the party, unless she is at death's door."

Sze Sze was at the party. So was Santa.

Despite the treatment—perhaps because of it—the infection was slow to heal, and Sze Sze continued to spend much time in her bedroom. On New Year's morning, while doing my cross stitch embroidery, we talked about family relationships. I told her about my childhood in Holland, my parents and brothers, our children and grandchildren and then moved on to her family. We talked about her mother, who visits her regularly, her brother, sister-in-law and nieces—Sze Sze is very proud of them but seldom gets to see them.

I then decided to talk about a touchy issue and said, "I don't know much about your father, Sze Sze, and I don't know if you want me to talk about him." Her face clouded over and she kept her tongue. "But do you think it is healthy never to talk about him, to harbor bitter thoughts about him and let those thoughts poison your life? Is it because he has abandoned you and the rest of the family that you hate him so?"

She looked angry when she answered yes.

I secured my needle, put down my embroidery and took her hand. "Not all fathers are alike, Sze Sze, some are very loving—my father was. I have noticed that the memory of your earthly father colors the way you think about God, your heavenly Father. You have trouble seeing him as loving. If I would have been your daddy, would your thoughts of God as a loving Father be different?" I watched her carefully. The hard expression in her eyes softened and a smile stole over her face. "In the past you've found it difficult to express your love for me properly. You love me more than a friend—and that's not wrong—but because of your bitter feelings for your own father, you have rejected the idea of loving me as my daddy, so you've tried to see me as a lover, which could never be." I paused to let her think about what I had said. "You haven't had a real father for a long time, have you, Sze Sze. I can never be your natural father, but I promise to be as loving as any real father *should* be . . . if only you let me."

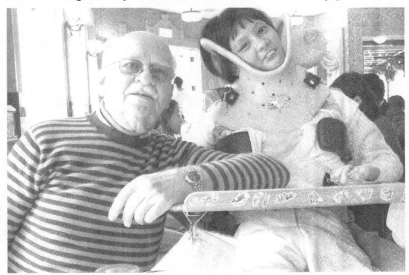

Sze Sze and Poh Poh

Sze Sze began to cry. Big tears coursed down her cheeks and onto her pillow, and deep sobs shook her body. I held her hand. I waited. When the tears stopped flowing, I took a tissue and wiped them away. She looked at me and a smile stole over her face. Her eyes filled with love. Then—softly—she said "Poh poh."

I bent over her, kissed her and whispered, "Happy New Year . . . daughter."

Epilogue

It's been more than six years since Sze Sze adopted me as her papa; it has made our relationship much more agreeable for both of us. Over the years, her love for me never wavered or diminished. It matured. At day's end, after doing devotions, after settling Sze Sze snugly for the night and after making sure there wasn't anything else she wanted me to do, it was heartwarming to hear her whisper Poh poh in response to my Goodnight, daughter.

As time passed, we cut back on instruction: we stopped spelling but continued our reading lessons. Sze Sze no longer stayed home from the center for instruction. At Uncle Pete's urging, the home invested in eye-gaze technology, but it, too, didn't work well for her. Sze Sze's uncontrolled head movements placed her eyes too often outside the range of the computer's camera, the instrument responding to the commands of her eyes, to have consistent and reliable results. Eventually, we fell back on the old way of communicating: asking questions.

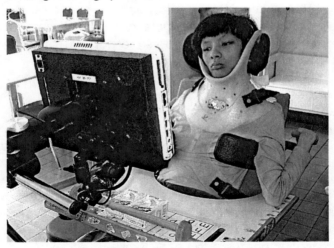

Sze Sze at her eye-gaze computer

Around that time, the Aunties decided to create a small family unit in the Lower Ark. Family members who would most appreciate such a change—Sze Sze, Dib Dib, Shaan Shaan and Fung Tai—moved to the Ark. Sze Sze and Dibs became roommates; they were by now the best of friends. Judy, a new volunteer, who had worked many years at Mothers' Choice, took charge of the newly created family unit. Moving a number of women from the C Block to the Ark allowed for another, much overdue change in the home, the separation of men and women. There was no longer any sharing of bedrooms by both sexes.

The move to the Ark was a wonderful change for Sze Sze and the others. They had their private or shared rooms, attractively furnished and tastefully decorated. There was also a large living room where they could hang out, listen to music or watch television or videos. In short, it was more like family. The change, however, was not without its problems. At Mothers' Choice, Judy had worked mainly with Down Syndrome children. They were able to walk and could be trained to dress, groom and feed themselves. Now she was in charge of physically disabled, wheelchair bound adults who needed full time care: bathing, diapering, dressing, grooming and feeding. Her adjustment to this new situation was challenging. It also took Sze Sze some time to feel at ease with Judy, leading to occasional conflicts, contentions that over time were resolved.

As Sze Sze got older, her abdominal problem—first manifesting itself when she was six months old, necessitating surgery to correct an obstruction, leading to cardiac arrest and resulting in her subsequent disability—became more pronounced and occurred at ever shorter intervals. The incidents did not always require surgical intervention, but they often resulted in hospital stays of one or more weeks. Doctors needed time to figure out how to keep her bowels moving, what combination of medications to prescribe or what method of feeding to recommend.

During one of those hospitalizations, it was determined that spoon feeding Sze Sze was no longer safe, and feeding by nasogastric tube[16] was ordered. They feared that choking on food might lead to aspirated pneumonia.[17] It was a decision that robbed her of the few pleasures left in life, the taste of food and the fellowship of the family around the table at mealtimes. Since it takes time for the plastic pouch to empty its content through the tube into her stomach, feeding was often started early, while Sze Sze was still sleeping—after all, she needed to be bathed, dressed and placed in her chair before the Rehabus came to collect her. The evening feeding, too, often took place in bed. Life for Sze Sze was beginning to lose its appeal.

Each hospitalization took some of Sze Sze's strength and spirit. I no longer witnessed any of the powerful extensions, and she gradually lost the interest and energy to cruise in her walker. Often, after coming home from the center at four, she wanted to go straight to bed. There I would find her, staring at the ceiling or watching the slow drip of the bag of Osmolite emptying, a mind-dulling and depressing exercise.

Our young friend went through a period when communication with her was difficult. Judy used to care for children for whom she had to make decisions. Now she needed time to get the measure of Sze Sze and get used to making decisions *with* rather than *for* her. Sze Sze often felt intimidated and confused. She was used to the way I communicated with her as equals. She began to give replies to queries by Judy, which, she hoped, would please her. However, when I asked her the same or similar questions, she would often answer differently. She knew that with me she could speak her mind and disagree. She was sure I would respect her opinion. When, in desperation, Judy would call in Wendy, Sze Sze's confusion increased. Not knowing which answer to give—the answer she had given Judy or me—she would sometimes give yet a different one. She felt trapped between different interests that, she felt, needed to be satisfied, pleased or appeased. No matter what we tried, we could not make her see she was creating serious problems for herself.

Each time Ena and I returned to Hong Kong, we noticed changes in Sze Sze. She was no longer the vivacious young woman, who showed an interest in all that happened around her. She lost interest in reading but enjoyed being read to, especially anything written by Joni Eareckson Tada. I spent many an hour at her bedside reading and discussing with her chapters from Joni's books. They spoke to her. She identified with Joni's struggles, especially her battles with sins of indulging in unhealthy daydreams. As Sze Sze's physical strength waned, I could see in her signs of spiritual growth.

Joni's books were such a blessing to Sze Sze, she asked me to write a letter, telling her what those books meant to her. We took a weekend to compose a letter. After a number of revisions, Sze Sze allowed me to mail the letter. A few weeks later, on Sze Sze's twenty-fifth birthday, a heavy, padded envelope, addressed to Miss

Chan Wing Sze, arrived at the Ark, with a personal letter from Joni and a copy of her book *Heaven, Your Real Home*.

When we returned to Hong Kong in the fall of 2010, Sze Sze seemed to be doing well. She appeared happy to see us, but I soon felt she wasn't as happy as she let on. Tube feeding sometimes caused her discomfort, but she felt not enough attention was paid to her complaints. Life was becoming increasingly boring and colorless for her. We were also receiving from caregivers the complaint that Sze Sze was becoming difficult. Four times within a relatively short time she had removed her nasogastric tube. When she was seated in her chair or lying in bed, her hands were restrained. To prevent the tube from being removed by her involuntary movements, her hands were tied to the sides of the wheelchair or to the bedrails. When she was bathed, however, her hands were free. The first time her hand flung out, hooked behind the tube and pulled it from her nostril, it was considered an accident. Then it happened a second, third and fourth time, and it became obvious that she was doing it deliberately. She was branded as becoming nasty and mean spirited and reprimanded for her actions. The next time she was bathed, however, she once again tried to remove her tube.

I knew Sze Sze. I knew it weren't frivolous reasons which had moved her to make life difficult for those who cared for her. I was convinced there was a deeper cause for her changed behavior. I took her to chapel and asked if she wanted to talk about it. She readily agreed. She admitted removing the tube deliberately but denied doing it to make life difficult for her care givers. When I asked her if she had done it to stop eating and starve herself, she began to weep softly. She admitted that was the case. I looked at her. My heart broke. What could I say? Here was a young woman, someone who enjoyed good food, being fed through a tube. Sometimes tube feeding caused her discomfort, and the medicine administered through the tube after her meal only intensified the pain. When she looks to the future, there is nothing to cheer her—just more of the same. She is looking forward to be delivered from this body of pain, but every time she is close to death, the portals of heaven are closed to her. Small wonder she wanted to give the Lord a hand in bringing an end to her suffering.

I gently reminded her that the Sixth Commandment includes those who kill themselves, that the gates of heaven are closed to all who take a life—someone else's or their own. We then read part of Psalm 139 where it says that all the days ordained for her are written in God's book. I told her that she must wait until those days are full. When I asked her if she wanted to be fed by mouth again, she managed a smile. I then asked her if she wanted me to talk to Judy and Wendy about this, explain why she had acted as she had done and tell them she wanted to get off tube feeding. She agreed to my plan.

A meeting was planned for the morning of November 3; Auntie Wendy, Judy, Sze Sze and I were present. Little attention was paid to Sze Sze's emotional state; instead she was admonished for her unacceptable behavior resulting from that condition. Her only comfort was the decision that, if the nurse in charge agreed, she would be spoon fed again. Before that decision could be made, however, Sze Sze was rushed to the Prince of Wales Hospital with severe abdominal pain. It was the morning of November 5, her twenty-sixth birthday.

We visited her that evening. She was in obvious distress: physically in pain, emotionally angry with the situation and with God and spiritually depressed. The following two and a half months became the most trying and painful period of her life. She relived the ordeal she had endured six years earlier. She underwent two surgeries and painfully slow recoveries—even the second surgery failed to solve Sze Sze's problems. Her bowels still refused to move, her abdomen continued to be distended and spasms of pain kept assaulting her at regular intervals.

Doctors were baffled. They were at a loss at how to restart peristalsis and alleviate pain. She was a sore sight to behold: two tubes protruded from infected areas in her abdomen to drain them; a catheter emptied her infected bladder; a nasal tube discharged bucketsful of green, noxious-looking juices from her intestines. Arms and legs were blotched by bruises, varying in color from yellow to green to blue, depending on how recently and successfully nurses had tried to insert intravenous and other needles. She needed several blood transfusions. When she had lost so much weight that she was hardly recognizable, intravenous feeding was replaced by a direct line in: a tube was inserted directly below her throat, through which a milky substance was pumped directly into one of her main arteries, but even then she continued to lose weight. Pain management was difficult; morphine dulled the pain at the site of incisions and infections but did little for the pain caused by colic.

One serious source of distress was her mouth. Because Sze Sze was not allowed to have anything by mouth, it was often very dry. She was also chesty and produced much phlegm. This mucous, perhaps mixed with foul stuff welling up from her stomach, dried in her mouth to a hard, black, crusty layer covering the inside of her mouth and sometimes her lips. Nurses seldom cleaned her mouth. When we entered the ward, we were at times greeted by a raw, agonizing cry. Then we knew what awaited us. While Ena straightened Sze Sze's bed, often in disarray because of her tossing and turning, and wiped her arm and legs with a damp flannel, I would go straight to work. Using oversized cotton swabs and boiled water, I cleaned her mouth. It would take thirty to forty-five minutes to get the job done. It was a painful procedure for Sze Sze, but it was the first thing she wanted me to do. I would then soften her cracked lips with olive oil, applying several applications during each visit. While I was cleaning her mouth, I would relate to her the latest gossip from the home, recite Scripture verses, pray—do anything to keep her mind off her agony. I then kept her mouth moist by dipping a clean flannel in Ribena juice and putting it in her mouth.[18]

For almost two and a half months, Ena and I spent two hours almost every day at Sze Sze's bedside. We watched her suffer, tried to alleviate her discomfort and give her emotional and spiritual support. We often felt helpless and frustrated we couldn't do more, and we reluctantly left at the end of visiting hours. On days when Judy could not make the noon time visit, we visited her twice. It was an emotionally draining time. When we reluctantly returned home to Canada one week before her discharge from the hospital, there was little left of our dear friend. She was severely emaciated and looked like a survivor of a Nazi extermination camp.

We returned in September of the same year and found a much changed Sze Sze. She was no longer a member of the Ark family; her bed had been placed directly beside the nurse's station in the C Block. Her nasogastric tube had been replaced by a stoma in her abdomen; through it, Osmolite was pumped directly into her jejunum[19]. She looked healthy and had regained whatever weight she had lost during her hospital stay. But something was missing—her lively spirit, her interest in her surroundings, her relish for things that make life worth living.

She was truly happy to see us again, and she enjoyed having me around, but she made no effort to interact with me as she had done in the past. I often found her either in bed or in her wheelchair, eyes closed, shutting out the world around her. Undoubtedly, one reason was her diminished level of energy, but I believe this was merely a contributing factor. There were other, more important causes for her apathy. Once again she had gone through a very traumatic period. It had brought her once more close to death—a death she had sought, wished and prayed for, a prayer that once again had gone unanswered. She also knew that, except on special occasions, she would never again enjoy the taste of good food. She also missed belonging to a small family group and the social interaction of the Ark community. Too many things had changed her small world in too short a period of time. It depressed her. I am not sure her caregivers noticed; they were too busy making beds, feeding mouths and changing nappies. I am sure the nurses did not realize; they had joined the staff rather recently and had not known the 'other' Sze Sze.

All people—hale and hearty or living with disabilities—have the same basic needs: a loving home, nourishing food, a clean and attractive wardrobe, personal hygiene and medical care. Those needs are well supplied by the home. But other things—less tangible—are needed, to make life worth living: emotional and spiritual support, entertainment and social interaction. Those of us who are able bodied can do much to satisfy our physical needs; we work, and with our earnings we satisfy them. As for our other needs, we call on a friend when we feel depressed or go to church to recharge our spiritual batteries; we go on a date when we want companionship or to a concert when we are bored. We can initiate actions to satisfy our needs and wants. Not so our disabled friends. Many of them are even unable to voice their needs. They lie in their beds or sit in wheelchairs. They wait for someone to notice them, to read their body language, to find out what their needs are and to give of themselves to satisfy those needs. Popping another CD or DVD into an electronic babysitter may bring temporary diversion but won't satisfy those deeper needs.

Was it because of staffing or financial considerations, rather than insensitivity or indifference that the emotional and social needs of Sze Sze and other members of the family were not always met? I like to think not. Were decisions on how personnel and financial resources should be allocated sometimes based on convenience or expedience rather than principle? I dare not make that assertion. I love the home, the people who live there and those who care for them. I have the deepest affection for the Aunties and the greatest respect for all they have done for those who cannot take care of themselves. It has earned them praise of all who care for the disabled in Hong Kong. I honor their faith and trust in God's providence that has motivated them. However, I would do the family—our special friends whom we love deeply—a disservice if I let my affections blind me to some of the shortcomings of the home. Those deficiencies could be remedied by having on staff one person who would be free from giving physical care, whose sole responsibility it would be to deal with the emotional and spiritual needs of the family and coordinate social activities. This may seem like a tall order to fill for one person, but she could use the services of staff and volunteers.

After almost forty-seven years of faithful service, Wendy Blackmur has retired from active service; Valerie Conibear, well into her eighties, has slowed down but finds it hard to quit. It is my prayer that Gretchen Ryan, the new superintendent of the Home of Loving Faithfulness, may build upon the solid foundation those two faithful servants have laid, and that she may provide for the continued welfare of the family those supports and services that I believe are lacking.

Someone wiser than I once wrote that there is a time and a season for every enterprise under heaven[20]—sage words worth savoring—but there are times in our lives, seasons rich in enjoyment and fulfillment, we would want to last a lifetime. However, advancing years and concerns about declining health have a way of bringing us back to reality. They remind us to hold loosely the things we prize and to let go of the things we cherish lest they become idols. They prod us to give thanks for the years we were privileged to enjoy them. While we were doing those things that gave meaning and purpose to our lives—serving the family at the Home of Loving Faithfulness—time took its toll and bid us slow down. We are trying, but we find adjusting to the pace of life in an assisted living community (our final station in the journey of life?) harder than we anticipated. We have much time to reminisce.

Now the time has come to reflect on the way we have spent our retirement years, to look back on our time of service in Hong Kong. Between December 2001 and January 2012, we traveled to Hong Kong sixteen times to work with the family. Sometimes I wonder what happened during those five days in December 2001, the first time Ena and I reluctantly visited the home. Neither Ena nor I was aware of an audible message from heaven, a flash of revelation or a special vision prompting us to volunteer our services. However, both of us believed then, and we still do today, that we were led there by Divine appointment. We feel it was the right thing for us to give of our time and energy, our abilities and love, in short, to give of ourselves and be a blessing to those who are completely dependent on others. In the process, we learned there is great joy in serving. While some of our friends took cruises up the Inside Passage to Alaska in summer, and others spent winter months in Southern California or sunny Arizona to escape the damp and dreary West Coast weather, we were feeding our kids oatmeal porridge for breakfast, wiping their lunches off our glasses and saliva off their chins and praying with them before they went to sleep. Although they were not able to tell us how much of a blessing we were to them, the joy on their faces, whenever they saw us or heard our voices, spoke more eloquently than words. God has so his own way of blessing those who bless others. Yes, these have truly been our golden years. If ever we have felt blessed in our almost eighty years, it has been during those last ten in Hong Kong.

We look back with gratitude on those years. First of all, Ena and I thank the Aunties for allowing us to return to the home time and again, for their trust in us, for their love for us, for making us feel part of the HOLLF family. We are grateful to the dedicated nurses, workers and caregivers who often went out of their way to include us in their social activities: their outings, barbecues and hot pot meals. Often, coming home from a hospital visit, tired and emotionally drained, we found Pui Yee or Ah Lee setting a table and preparing a hot meal for us—thanks, dear friends. You have no idea how much we needed that loving gesture in those days. Then there was Kim, quiet, almost reclusive, always ready to make one more trip to collect us from the airport or bring us back; and Lita in the laundry room, no matter how swamped with buckets of laundry, always willing to wash our clothes and have them neatly folded by the end of the day; and Priscilla in the office, dedicated to her duties, but never too busy to answer a question, find an address or supply us with whatever information we needed; and Belen, cheerfully boisterous, dedicated and warmhearted, modeling what it means to be a servant; and Judy, forever trying to keep one step ahead of things, yet including Sze Sze in as many social activities in the Ark as possible and Skyping us most weekends so we can talk to our kids; and all the other wonderful unnamed people serving the family—a big thank you to all for making us feel we belonged.

Sze Sze, thank you for allowing me to be part of your life. You let me probe your thoughts and feelings; you had the courage to say no when I asked questions I had no right to ask; and you trusted me to tell your story to the world. You allowed me to let others know how much you, and others like you, are like us: having the same needs and desires and deserving to be treated with the same dignity and respect. Thank you for graciously forgiving me for not always delivering what I had hoped to accomplish. Thank you for loving this old man and adopting him as your daddy.

Finally, I thank my heavenly Father for leading us to the Home of Loving Faithfulness, for the privilege of serving his special image bearers, for using them to teach us to love the way He loves us—unconditionally, and blessing us richly in the process.

Abbotsford, British Columbia, July 2012

Endnotes

Chapter 1
[1] Sze Sze – pronounced She She. Her full name is Chan Wing Sze. In Chinese names, the family name (Chan) comes before the given name (Wing Sze). The repetition of a name in Chinese, as in Sze Sze, Fa Fa, Fu Fu, etc., is a form of endearment.
[2] The Chinese name for their country is *Zhongguo*. It means Middle Kingdom.
[3] *lao shi* – teacher
[4] *tai tai* – wife
[5] Golden Week – A week of festivities, beginning October 1, celebrating China's National Day. It was on 1 October 1949, that Mao Ze Dong declared the establishment of the Peoples' Republic of China.

Chapter 2
[6] William Henry Davies (1871–1940), British poet. *Leisure*, Songs of Joy (1911).
[7] Linda Ball, *Secret Riches,* p. 149, Living Books for All, CLC Ministries International, 2005
[8] Paul Laurence Dunbar (1872–1906), U.S. poet. *Sympathy*, Poetry of the Negro, 1746–1970. Langston Hughes and Arna Bontemps, eds. (Rev. ed., 1970) Doubleday & Company.

Chapter 3
[9] Henry David Thoreau (1817–1862), U.S. philosopher, author, naturalist. *Walden* (1854), in The Writings of Henry David Thoreau, vol. 2, p. 356, Houghton Mifflin (1906).

Chapter 4
[10] Following the English tradition, English speaking people in Hong Kong call the evening meal tea.

Chapter 5
[11] 1 July 1997, the date Hong Kong reverted to China

Chapter 6
[12] *Putonghua* – Mandarin

Chapter 9
[13] A free translation by the author of the following Dutch poem:
Een mens lijdt dikwijls 't meest
Door 't lijden dat hij vreest
Doch dat nooit op komt dagen.
Zo heeft hij meer te dragen
Dan God te dragen geeft.

Chapter 11
[14] *Fa* is Cantonese for flower

Chapter 12
[15] From Ivor Novello's song, *We'll Gather Lilacs*

Epilogue
[16] nasogastric tube - A tube inserted in one of the nostrils, passing through the esophagus into the stomach

[17] aspirated pneumonia - Pneumonia caused by food inhaled into the respiratory system.

[18] In the past, Sze Sze had been cared for in the older part of the Prince of Wales Hospital. Nurses were kind and considerate and treated her with care and dignity. This time she was in the newly opened twelve-story surgical and trauma center. We didn't recognize any of the nurses who had worked with her in the old ward. The treatment of Sze Sze by the nurses in the new section left much to be desired.

[19] jejunum - The middle portion of the small intestine, between the duodenum and the ileum

[20] Ecclesiastes 3:1

CPSIA information can be obtained at www.ICGtesting.com
Printed in the USA
LVOW040800130912

298561LV00002B/1/P